A Little Course in Dreams

Also by Robert Bosnak

Dreaming with an AIDS Patient
A Little Course in Dreams (audio tape) from Shambhala Lion Editions

A Little Course in Dreams

Robert Bosnak

FOREWORD BY
Denise Levertov

SHAMBHALA
Boston & London
1988

Shambhala Publications, Inc.
Horticultural Hall
300 Massachusetts Avenue
Boston, Massachusetts 02115

A *Little Course in Dreams* was translated from the Dutch by Michael H.
Kohn and the author. The original book, *Kleine droomcursus,* was published
by Lemniscaat, Rotterdam.

9 8 7 6

Printed in the United States of America on acid-free paper ⊗

Distributed in the United States by Random House, Inc., and in Canada by
Random House of Canada, Litd.

Library of Congress Cataloging-in-Publication Data
Bosnak, Robert.
    [Kleine droomcursus. English]
    A little course in dreams / Robert Bosnak.
        p.   cm.
    Translation of: Kleine droomcursus.
    ISBN 0-87773-451-8 (pbk.)
    1. Dreams.   I. Title.
    BF1078.B57613   1988   88-15870
    154.6'34—dc19   CIP

To Eranos

CONTENTS

FOREWORD

Anyone who has ever dreamed could find this book of interest—and those who declare they "never dream" will encounter a practical method of dream-retrieval. People already engaged in dream work will obtain fascinating insights into the way dreams, like poems, can intensify and sometimes clarify a sense of life.

Robert Bosnak permits the reader to enter his own experience both as dreamer and as "creative listener" to the dreams of others. For the lay reader, his candor and a lucid and vivacious style of expression impart a new concreteness to terms like "resistance" or "transference," or to distinctions such as that between "free association" and "active imagination." Alchemical concepts in psychology are illustrated in dramatic reconstructions of workshop sessions. Of interest to writers will be the sidelights on the nature of metaphor which are emitted by Bosnak's account of his own associative perceptions—and it is of particular interest to the general reader to obtain this inside view of the process by which a gifted analyst arrives at the interpretive recognitions by which analysands are awakened to their own recognition of dream significance. And over and above the fascination of this study on an individual level, Bosnak leads the reader to perceive the importance to society, the *political* value, of increasing our attention to those powerful aspects of our being that go uncomprehended in the ignored dreamlife of billions.

DENISE LEVERTOV

A Little Course in Dreams

Driving In

I am sitting in the car on my way to Cambridge, Massachusetts, where I have my analytical practice. The commuter traffic goes by fits and starts, which gives me time to quietly contemplate last night's dream.

I dreamt the following:

> I am in a house under construction. There is a beautiful great Saint Bernard dog, called Angie, who is being attacked by a bulldog I have on a leash. The bulldog bites Angie's neck, holding her there, and they disappear together, engaged in a deadly fight. I am frightened. When Angie reappears, rather disheveled but apparently unharmed, I am very happy. The bulldog has disappeared. After this I am at the wedding of the son of my most ambitious and power-hungry uncle.

Now I have to stop for a stoplight, and the Boston drivers, who all seem to have the right of way at the same time, demand my complete attention.

Not until I am in my consulting room do I get the time to reflect on the dream some more. I still have ten minutes before my first patient. The kettle whistles; tea has been made. Now

I'm sitting in my rocking chair, staring at the rocking chair opposite me.

There, across from myself, I sit: my first patient. From one rocking chair to the other I tell my dream to myself as analyst. The first thing that occurs to me is how much my uncle looks like a tenacious bulldog whose power-hunger eats and corrodes everything. I can feel his power-hunger in my jaws, and I clench them together until they hurt. Then I growl. Suddenly I lunge for Angie's throat and see blood before my eyes. Terrible rage. Vampire in the neck. Keep on biting, kill that animal! I associate:

Angie, angel. I don't know any Angie. I've never seen that dog before, even though she was very familiar to me in the dream. Angie? Yes, of course! A long time ago. She sang like an angel. Angel? My wife . . . anger with her? My mother? My daughter? Incest-rage? Sure. But that I've known for a long time. That doesn't surprise me at all. For that I don't need this dream.

Bulldog. I've been told that bulldogs are specially bred to never let go when they sink their teeth into something. My first patient, who will be on my doorstep in seven minutes, looks like a bulldog. He bites whatever he can—particularly women. He wants to dominate them. And I have that bulldog on a leash. Or he is stringing me along. What a mess.

"Yech, I'd better stop thinking."

"You'd better think on!" my analyst says strictly, catching me like a bad schoolboy.

Angie? Angie? Angel! That's the only thing constantly emerging from within. The only thing left is to return to the memory of what happened in the dream. I try to recall the dream image in as much detail as possible. After a while I can clearly see her standing before me again. Such a gorgeous dog! A beautiful, humongous animal. The head is the image of beauty. But what kind of image? And who was Saint Bernard, really? I should look that up tonight. Now I think of rescue dogs who carry medicine kits around their necks and dig stranded travelers out of the snow. Stranded travelers. Have I stranded? Where have I stranded? My healing angel. . . . I look at my watch. What a pity; just five minutes left. I hope the bull-dog will be late today. But that won't happen. If you really want people to be late, they're always on time.

The more I look at Angie, the more lucid she becomes and the more beautiful I think she is. I find myself ogling her like a lovesick teenager. And a dog no less; how perverted! But she's not just any old dog. No, now I see her as an inspiring being full of power and grace. A powerful female animal. Power, powerful. My power-hungry uncle reigns supreme on this day of marriage. Two opposite kinds of power: one is the beautiful female power of images, which brings healing, the other a grim, biting masculine rapist who has me on a leash. He rapes my angel, tries to overpower her. He is a pain in the neck. He wants to take possession of my angel. Maybe to make money off her. My uncle makes money off anything. To use the Muse to write books. Like this book, this house under con-struction. Become famous, have power. The voice of the bull-dog now sounds almost hysterically power-hungry.

Thank God Angie returns alone, apparently victorious. But of course I know that dreams are not linear stories, with a beginning and an end, once and for all. Dreams are patterns that return constantly in ever-shifting tones. The battle between my rescuing guardian angel and the devouring bite of the bulldog is far from over. It is one of the structures of my soul that presents itself in ever-new forms. Sometimes I'm consciously more on one side of the battle, sometimes more on the other. The struggle expresses itself in many different ways.

I should ask my wife tonight whether I sometimes attack her like a bulldog and if I abreact my fury at women on her. But maybe she'll seize the chance to vent all of her anger at me; and who knows, if she doesn't like me at that particular moment (any deep relationship has its bitterness), she'll tell me that I always behave like a bloody hound. I should think twice before I give her all that ammunition.

Now I'm staring at both dogs, letting their character qualities sink in. In its own way, each dog belongs to me as I belong to it.

The doorbell rings.

First patient.

He is fighting with his girlfriend again. I see how he grinds his jaws as if he were biting. He is jealous of any man she looks at. "Damnit, she should stop looking at men," he yells, furious.

"That's easy," I remark; "all you have to do is take a knitting needle and poke her eyes out. Quite effective and permanent. She'll never look at another man again."

This remark came out of me entirely unexpected. We're both startled. At first we nervously giggle a little, as if we've both been caught at something. Finally we're both disgusted and forced to reflect.

With each of his most intimate girlfriends, mother included, he's felt this same jealousy, especially when his work is stagnant. He's a writer. When he is blocked, he believes that he somehow has to get his inspiration under control, and he becomes furious because nothing is coming out of his hands. On top of this he's been out of work for months. Money is running out and sex isn't fun anymore either. He feels powerless, impotent, and furious. Whose dream was it, that dream of the dogs? My dream or his?

A new day has begun. Begun in a dream of a house under construction. Or was it demolition? Suddenly I can't remember it very well. My own images become increasingly vague as I am thrown as by a slingshot with full force into someone else's soul, mangled between propulsion and repulsion.

– 1 –

Memory Exercises

A dream is not a story, not a movie or text or a theater play. A dream is a happening in space, an articulation of space.

We find ourselves in a space we call "dream" upon awakening. In that space we experience things we can talk about upon awakening as a dream story. But the dream story is not the dream itself. The dream itself is a texture woven of space and time inside which we find ourselves. During the dream we believe we are awake, in the same way that we believe we are awake when we truly are. That's why it is important to remember dreams as spatial structures, so that our experiences in dream space can be most adequately recalled.

Memory existed before it was measured in kilobytes. In classical antiquity memory was seen as a spatial reality, and therefore the storage of memory facts took place in a space. The orators of ancient Rome learned to develop their memory by moving through a memory warehouse. Such a warehouse came to life in the following way.

One could see the orators walk through an empty building, dressed in togas. They were concentrating very carefully on each aspect of the space around them. They would do this until they knew each nook and cranny by heart. After this space had been implanted firmly in memory, it could serve as a storage room for things to be recalled. Now, for instance, a five-hundred-line poem must be remembered. At the first step to the right, at the point where the marble is slightly yellow, the first line is deposited. At the third step to the right, line two; and at a pillar (the one with the red vein in the marble) on top of the stairs, line three. In this way memory facts could be stored at each specific point inside the building. And by way of an imaginary walk through the warehouse, each sentence could be picked up again in the correct order. The creation of an imaginary space helps spatial recall. And it is just this development of spatial recall that is crucial in the work on dreams.

The following exercises have been developed from these ancient mnemonics, this art of memory.

EXERCISE 1
Moving through the Dream World

Look around and see where you are. Look around and know that you are awake. Now realize that you also think that you are awake when you are dreaming. Now know that you feel you are awake but that this does not mean that you are not dreaming.

When you have called this realization up into consciousness, proceed from the viewpoint that you are in fact dreaming.

You find yourself in a dream world that surrounds you entirely, as it does every night. It is a world that is utterly authentic. Touch the ground: it is firm. Pinch your arm. How does that feel?

Now begin to move through the space. You continue to know that you are moving around inside an ordinary nightly dream, while at the same time you're certain that you're awake. Look intensively at each object around you.

Repeat this exercise often.

EXERCISE 2
Recalling Dream Objects

You are dreaming that you are learning memory exercises from a book called A *Little Course in Dreams*. Now you take this book between both hands and carefully study what it looks like. Then you slowly rotate the book one full turn, while watching it intently as a slowly rotating object.

Close your eyes.

Now look inside your memory again at the book as object. Try to recall how it rotated and what it looked like from different angles.

Repeat this exercise with several different objects.

EXERCISE 3
Creating a Memory Storage Room

Find a space where you can walk around within a range of several yards: for instance, a room where several objects stand out. Walk around in this room for a while. Etch each nook and cranny deeply into your memory. Then sit or lie down, close your eyes, and recall each detail again before your inner eye. The more often you do this, the easier it gets. Some objects can be more easily recalled by touching them with your hands or smelling them. Coordinate your senses as much as possible in this imprinting process.

Like the orators of old, you now have a memory storage room.

An Imaginary Tour of Your House

Move through your memory and find the house of which you have the clearest recollection: for example, your parental home or the house in which you now live. Take a moment to imagine a few well-known houses, and decide which one you can imagine best at this particular instant.

After you've read the following paragraphs, close your eyes and concentrate for a minute on your breathing. Feel how your breath goes through your lungs, and become aware of as many bodily sensations as you can observe. Start with your feet and move upward slowly. At the moment that you've felt your way deeply into your body, visualize the house you want to enter in imagination. Look at the front of the house, or wherever the doorway is that is your usual entrance to the house. Look at it carefully. Observe the details. Are there windows? What colors are the building materials (wood, masonry, stones, and so on)? Observe carefully. Then turn your back to the doorway and look around. What do you see in front of you? Now turn around slowly until you are facing the doorway again. If there is a door, what does it look like? How high is it? What color is it? Where is the doorknob, the doorbell?

Now open the door and stand on the threshold. Look around. Let your eyes get used to the possible change of light, and look at the floor. What does the floor look like? Stone?

Wood? What? Keep imagining, even if your memory gets stuck. What do the walls look like? Look up. The ceiling? Now begin to move slowly through the space that you're in and, if you're not in the kitchen, go there. *Make sure you walk slowly.* Take your time. Look around constantly, up, down, in front of you, behind you, to your left and your right. If you see an interesting object, go to it and look at it.

In the kitchen, go to the sink. Is there a faucet? What does it look like? What is below the sink? Is there a stove or some other cooking apparatus? Gas, electric, wood? What is there between the stove and the sink? What does the floor look like? Are there any windows? Look up; any light fixtures? Now take your time to look around without haste and find interesting objects you would like to take a closer look at.

When you've looked around extensively, you *slowly* move to that place in the house where your bed is. Slowly, much more slowly. Slowing down is one of the most difficult exercises in the volatile world of images.

Now you're standing in front of your bed and you're looking around. What does the space around your bed look like? Again, look around in all directions, above you and below you. Observe your bed carefully. Go and sit on the side of your bed. Then lie down on it. Slowly! If there are blankets, get under them. Now close your eyes and remember how you used to feel in this bed. Stay like that for a little while, until you can exactly recall the feelings that belong to this bed. Then slowly sit up and look around you. Has anything changed in the surrounding area? Look down, up, behind you, in front of you.

Now slowly get up and move at a snail's pace to the door through which you entered. Look around. See if anything has changed since you've entered. Then open the door (if it was closed) and go out. Stand with your back to the door, and slowly wake up in the place where you're sitting with this book. Attentively observe the transition from image consciousness to waking consciousness.

The next exercises are about recording dreams. Recording dreams in writing is of great importance. Just think how many dreams you've had that you were positive you would never forget, never in your entire life. Yet after a few minutes, or sometimes seconds, they disappeared untraceably from consciousness. The recording of dreams is an effort to counteract this evaporation. A recorded dream is a memory support through which you can often find your way back to the dream again. Sometimes it is the only thing that remains from a dream, like hieroglyphics on the ruins of a culture that passed away, a notation on a gravestone from days long gone.

Some people say that they never dream. That is an incorrect statement. They should say that they don't *remember* their dreams. Laboratory dream research has established the fact that everyone has about five dream periods per night. During the dream the eyes move very rapidly behind the closed eyelids. This is called REM (rapid eye movement) sleep. Everyone has about five REM periods a night—far too many dreams to remember. The transition from dreaming consciousness to waking consciousness, however, is by way of oblivion. The question is, how can we catch a dream before it evaporates?

EXERCISE 5
Observing the Moment of Awakening

Begin with the intention of waking up as consciously as possible. Try to really experience the transition between sleeping and waking. When you wake up, *before* your alarm goes off, remain exactly in the position you're in and observe the way sleeping transits to waking. Feel how your body wakes up. Where are the tensions? How does your head feel? Your breathing? And so on. Do this every day for a week and decide absolutely to remember *no dreams whatsoever*. The only thing that matters is observing the moment of waking.

EXERCISE 6
Preparing to Record Your Dreams

After completing the week in exercise 5, put a notepad and pen next to your bed. See to it that a *weak* light is within reach; it should be just strong enough to enable you to read your own handwriting. Or you could put a voice-activated tape recorder next to your bed. This is a dubious method of recording dreams, however, because it puts an extra step between the dream and the written recording. Internal resistances can keep you from writing down the taped dreams, and finally you have several hours of mumbling and no text.

Now repeat the previous exercise, while at the same time being conscious that a writing pad is patiently waiting next to your bed. Try not to remember any dream. If one comes through anyway, write it down.

EXERCISE 7
Writing Down Your Dreams

If dream recall is no problem for you, then start here. There are several methods of recording, of which I will describe three.

1. You wake up with a shred of a dream that is still vaguely fluttering behind. Remain very quietly in the same position, like a hunting dog observing its prey. Don't jump at the dream immediately, but look at it for a moment. Then, with closed eyes, grab the pen and write down exactly what you remember of this shred. Then stop again. Let your attention float alongside this image. Often another image of the same dream emerges. Write it down. From that point on you can often reel in the entire dream.

2. You wake up in the middle of the night with an entire dream and the feeling that there is so much to it that you can't possibly write it all down. In that case, first record the most salient details of the dream with a few short descriptive words, for a memory support. For instance, "Construction, Saint Bernard Angie, bulldog, fight, neck, gone, afraid. Return, happy." Then go back to sleep. If, in the morning, you haven't the foggiest idea what these code words refer to, it's gone wrong. In case you do remember, move through the images as you did in the imaginary tour through your house (exercise 4), and try to write down each detail more or less legibly. Many dreams disappear into illegibility.

3. You wake up in the morning with a dream. You begin

–14–

with writing down the last scene, and you write your way back to the beginning. Or just go from the beginning to the end. Don't dwell too much on the story line, or you might lose the details of the images. It is ideal to describe the images from *inside* them, so that you just have to look around.

In the shower and during breakfast you imprint the dream deeply into your memory. If you feel like it, you might tell it to someone. When you do, you often remember things that had remained outside your vision before. In telling the dream, there is already a mirroring taking place, without any comment from the other person. An outside ear changes the perspective. You learn the dream by heart as if it were a poem. The dream will start giving off words, like fragrances, as you muse about it. In this way you maintain access to your dreams throughout the day. Every time you go to the bathroom or when you're alone for a moment, very briefly enter the dream. Remember each detail. Then at night, just before you go to sleep, move through the dream once more.

Good night.

Don't select your dreams before you write them down. Resistances often make a dream seem trivial at first glance; after some mining work, these apparently insignificant dreams often yield a lot of material. Sometimes people don't write down those dreams that would be disapproved of by others (parents, spouse, suspected snoopers: "I always have the feeling that someone is peeking into my dream book when I'm not around"). Together with Saint Augustine, thank the Higher Powers who have made us not responsible for our dreams, and write down those dreams especially.

Never believe that you will remember this dream forever and therefore you don't have to write it down. After five minutes this "eternal" memory may have disappeared.

EXERCISE 8
Dealing with an Overabundance of Dream Material

Now we get to the opposite problem of "I never dream," namely, "I have so many dreams that I could be writing them down all night and I'd be walking through each day with seven new dreams."

In analysis it sometimes happens that analysands come in with so much dream material that we don't get to anything else. Sometimes this is a resistance phenomenon in which the essential material disappears behind the opulence. Usually the dream memory adjusts to the quantity that can be handled by daytime consciousness. If for some reason this is not the case, it makes no sense to me to totter through the day with bloodshot eyes and rubber knees because you've been up all night writing down dreams. In that case, remember two dreams, period. If more come up and there is one that offers itself with exceptional vigor and conviction, adopt that one in your dream book. The other dreams will have to remain orphans.

If you do these exercises like a schoolchild who is obliged to do make-up work over the summer, and if you get a frown every time you don't complete them, you've landed in an image that will create many resistances. Always be aware from whose perspective you are doing these exercises. Are you

–16–

doing them as a Sherlock Holmes, as an apprentice in mysticism, as a self-healer, as a researcher?

Dreamwork is surrounded by resistances. This often causes some kind of aversion to the work. Try to feel the resistances as deeply as you can. They may express themselves as repulsion, boredom, the feeling of being involved in something utterly insignificant, or the feeling of being ridiculous. Don't try to fight these resistances; just observe them. Give them as much space as they want. Learning to sense resistances is much more important than eliminating them.

– 2 –

A Dream Text

Now that we have clearly established the fact that there is a vast difference between a dream and a dream story—as vast as the difference between a story in the newspaper and the actual event that it describes—let us occupy ourselves with a recorded dream, a dream text.

You've put a pen next to your bed, on your night table, close to the dim light, just bright enough to write by, and you've caught a dream. It didn't slip through your fingers, and you've been able to write it down quickly in the middle of the night. Now it is the next morning, and you can still clearly recall several images, but others don't return when you read the dream text you've hurriedly jotted down in a nocturnal scribble. Such a half-evaporated dream happens often: a dream that consists partly of living images that can be reexperienced and partly of recorded reports of a vanished era, a forgotten dream.

What can we do with these reports, these dream texts? As my point of departure, I take a dream to be a psychic organism, a living reality in spatial form. One cannot remove an organ from a human being without altering the entire body, and the same is true of a dream image. All the constituent elements of a dream image belong to the identity of the dream. Each part is necessary for the existence of that specific dream image.

A dream image is a complex construction, consisting of

different parts. Let's start with an image of a dream of one of my patients, whom I'll call Stella: "I'm a prisoner in a plane which has glass bottom." This opening image of the dream text consists of five parts: I, prisoner, plane, glass, bottom. These five components are present simultaneously and can be interconnected in various ways.

The words *plane* and *bottom* have double meanings. *Plane* means "airplane" and also "level." *Bottom* means "underside" and also "buttocks." These are double meanings in the language that thus belong to the context as well.

- My imprisonment exists in the fact that I look down on the world from a lofty position behind glass.
- I am like a prisoner on this flight with glass buttocks; flighty.
- On my high level there is glass between me and the visible world below my level. I am tied to this state like a prisoner.
- My flying spirit is bound to being distant.
- When my glass buttocks are in flight, fleeing, I feel like a prisoner; I am prisoner of this "flight of the glass buttocks," caught in the high speed.

I'm trying to create new images from the simultaneous image elements. As I shuffle the image elements like a deck of cards, vague hunches begin to develop. The figurative meaning of the images, the metaphor, begins to stand out. This is the processing of the raw dream text until it yields metaphor. For this it is also necessary to bring to the surface the specific qualities of each image component. This can be done by asking the dreamer for associations to certain images; for example, "What comes up when you think of airplanes?" This leads to associative networks that are directly or tangentially related to the dream image, such as, "Last week I was on a plane to . . ." or "When I was small, I had a fear of flying" or "My aunt is a pilot."

Asking for associations is one of the essential parts of work on dreams. It makes for connections between the dream and daily life of the dreamer.

Next to these personal associations, each word creates a kind of electromagnetic field of meaning that is usually associated with that word. After the personal associations we can enter the fields surrounding the words.

- I—the self-image with which I usually identify, from which I respond to the world, and which I usually believe myself to be.
- Prisoner—locked up, restricted, locked in, inside something you can't get out of, introverted, closed, walled in, separated.
- Plane—flying through the air, great speed, created by rational ingenuity, propelled by controlled explosion, distant, being in flight; level, flat surface, two-dimensional.
- Glass—near-invisible separation, observation without being exposed to what is being observed, separated from the immediacy of events, seeing through but not sensing, transparent, fragile.
- Bottom—underside, lower parts, low, interface with below; behind, buttocks, sexual organs.

This dream image gives the impression of an I-figure who, locked into herself, feels restricted; who distantly looks down upon the lower world, feeling fragile and not really part of the immediacy of life; someone who, walled off from vitality, is driven by ingenious speed, airily looking down on others, someone in flight from her delicate sexuality, while constantly feeling exposed as a person whose contact with down-to-earth reality is easily shattered.

EXERCISE 9
Shuffling Dream Components

Make as many connections among the individual components (I, prisoner, plane, glass, bottom) as you can. You've just read one of the many possibilities for such shuffling. The more time you spend on it, the clearer the image becomes. Do this exercise in writing and make it the basis for reading the whole dream, of which this image is the initial situation.

Here is the text of the entire dream as the dreamer recorded it:

> I'm a prisoner in a plane which has glass bottom—
> we're crashing—out of control—I ask 2 other
> women in room to hold hands and meditate. One
> does. We are very calm about imminent death. We
> land and many people there—derelict types—
> someone nods letting me know that what I'm think-
> ing is true—we all are up for grabs for sex. One
> woman finds a cleaner man (I think in military) and
> will go to bed with him. She finds a man for me. He's
> in white—like Al Huang—probably a Dr. I'm at-
> tracted and so is he. He's smiling and easy to be with.
> I'm not threatened. I say I must wash first—hard

time—water spills over—I pea in shower with wooden floor—can't turn off water, etc. Someone comes for me. I'm afraid the man will be mad because we took too long—we look for him and he's in his room 3 or 4 stories up (we see light on).

One of the aims in working on dreams is connecting the images with the personal life of the dreamer. Earlier we looked at the initial image of this dream. Expressions like "distant" and "in flight" reverberate with the life of the dreamer. Four years ago Stella's relationship with her husband broke down after a sexually very active marriage. Since that time she has lived alone and has had no intimate relationships. Now in her early forties, she has been working with me for two years. After she left her husband, she became a college professor.

A certain degree of distance stood in the way of intimate relationships for Stella. She had no sex life and spent her days teaching, studying, and meditating several hours per day. Apparently the dream portrays a situation of being imprisoned above the level of everyday life. Stella looks at the world from behind glass and has no intimate contact (glass buttocks) on this elevated level. Then the situation crashes. Flying seems to give her a feeling of control over her existence, because at the moment flight stops she has a sense of being "out of control."

Before we go any further, imagine this scene: You're sitting in an airplane that is going down. What do you feel? Your whole life is collapsing—you feel as if you've lost control of the wheel. Crashing; falling; fear of heights. Death!

The I-figure in Stella's dream is very calm and quiet. Icy-calm, I would say. Generally, the I-figure is an aspect of habitual consciousness. That is, it reflects a person's habitual reactions and attitudes. The reason I do not call this I-figure "the dreamer" is that at the moment of dreaming, the dreamer and the dream are identical. The dream *is* the dream. The I-consciousness is only an aspect of the dream world and the dreamer.

"Yes," Stella says in an association regarding this calm I, "death doesn't frighten me at all. It is a continually recurring element in my meditation."

Stella's self-knowledge coincides here with the reactions of the I-figure.

The dream, however, gives an ambivalent picture. There are two female figures with whom Stella's I-figure wants to go hand in hand. In this meditative crash into swiftly impending death, Stella can only maintain contact with one of these figures. She can keep her hand on one of the women; the Other Woman underscores her independence of Stella by not giving her a hand. This turns out to be important later on, because the Other Woman knows how to deal with the world below.

We land on solid ground in the Land of Many People, people in the collective sense. A world of seedy characters. A motley crew. Drunkards, souses. Degradation. Here everything has been brought low, dragged through the mud. The world as dung heap, a filthy world. (Now I understand why she was protected/imprisoned behind glass on a lofty flight.) All kinds of filth, foulness, and dirt are combined, followed by sex.

In describing the image from the inside out, Stella paints

a world of dilapidated slums with filth on the streets and un-shaven men reeling drunkenly through the alleyways.

Then there is a figure that nods. She can't remember the figure clearly. Only the nod.

The Greek word for "nod" is *numen*. In Greek mythol-ogy, a deity betokens his or her overwhelming reality through a nod. From *numen* derives the English word *numinous*, which signifies the irrational aspect of the sacred, the mysterious god-liness that fascinates us and causes us to tremble.

The irrational mystery that makes Stella tremble is sex. "We are all up for grabs for sex." Grabbed by sex. Sexual capti-vation is imaged here. In the face of this captivation, the I-figure is powerless, overwhelmed. The high-flying habitual "I" is disabled. This is the world of captivation by sexuality in its dirty aspect. Everything here is filthy and foul, seedy and un-washed, intoxicating, besotting. This is the frequently de-scribed primordial image of the unrestrained life of the passions. At this point the search for a cleaner man begins, a search for purity in this repulsive venereal world. The indepen-dent Other Woman can obviously get along fine in this murky world. The Other Woman finds a relationship in this sinister place. She is militant and finds the soldier. Stella has scarcely any associations regarding the soldier. She just says, "War, a warrior who can fight. A knight who will protect her." The knightly man who can protect her in the skirmishes of sex. A similar figure appears for Stella—the Doctor in White.

Sex with the Doctor in White. He looks like Al Huang, a famous Chinese T'ai Chi teacher. In one of the workshops where I worked on this dream, many of the participants associated Al Huang with "wang," meaning penis. "El Wang." The healing phallus.

This healing sex, this sexual doctoring, happens through the exotic doctor. The exotic doctor takes away the threatening element and makes sex white, pure, and attractive.

Thus, by means of the Other Woman, a change has been brought about in the sexual experience. Now it can be doctored.

At this point it becomes clear that this dream contains elements of transference. Insofar as the Knight and the Doctor are experienced in the analyst, they are identified with the person of the analyst. From this an unconscious role-play can develop. In the language of analysis such role-play is called transference and countertransference. Often this imagined relationship is of a sexual nature. Now the water ballet begins.

It's a juicy mess—an overflow of unstoppable libido. Turn on. You can turn on the faucet, but once it's on you can't turn it off. Stella wants to get clean—to be purified. The sexual doctoring should take place in neat and proper cleanliness. But she can't hold back her surging impulses. They flood over her to such an extent that she pees on the wooden floor. She is full of juice, overfull. Stella wrote "pea" and not "pee." (Freud has taught us that slips in writing and speaking are of particular importance.) What does the image "pea" mean in this context? Recall the story of the princess and the pea. She was so sensitive that any irregularity in her bed would keep her up all night. She couldn't sleep because of a pea under twelve mattresses. The world of the lowly pea irritates the world of the princess.

This image of the pea adds a hypersensitive tendency to the image of fragile elevatedness in which the plane imprisoned Stella. The lofty princess-nature, so highly sensitive, holds aloof (many mattresses thick) from the world of little irritations, low down to the ground and exciting.

Who is the Oriental doctor with whom Stella must make love?

The doctor lives on the third or fourth floor. Three or four up. In these lowlands of sex, he lives above. He is an interplay of above and below, participating in both realities. He is the inoculation that is going to protect Stella from the all-too-direct attack of this lewd and seedy world. His sexual penetration will pervade her with sex. Homeopathically, he makes it possible for this dark underworld into which she has fallen not to rape and destroy her and yet to penetrate her. He vaccinates her. He is a light in a murky world ("We see light on"). Orient—orientation; a sense of direction in the dark world of sexual passion. Intimacy has become possible again after a long period of distance.

– 3 –

Listening to Dreams

My usual first reaction after listening to a dream is, "I haven't the faintest idea what this is all about. It just proves that dreams are pure nonsense—or maybe my comprehension is just not up to the complexity of the dream world." At such a moment I feel like a charlatan, an interpreter who hasn't mastered his languages, a con man. In short, I feel terribly inferior. Dreams seem incomprehensible by nature, nonsensical, an insult to "common sense." If I don't react in this way, however—if I immediately know precisely what the dream is all about—then I usually presume I'm caught in a resistance, trying to make the dream harmless by understanding it right away. A dream is not at home in our daytime consciousness. Like Mercury, the god of thieves, we have stolen the dream from its nocturnal domain. Every dream requires a switchover into a dreamlike consciousness that can follow the dream world. This switchover into dream consciousness is a shock. Daytime consciousness stumbles when confronted with a kind of logic that is *essentially* alien to it.

This stumbling of rational consciousness is a painful event, surrounded by a multitude of resistances. Nobody likes to stumble, and the dream trips us up. Thus, directly translating a dream into daytime logic using preconceived parallels is a method that does not do justice to the discrepancy between dream reality and daytime reality and is therefore fundamentally inadequate.

One of the tasks in working on dreams is to trip up our daytime consciousness again and again in order to unhinge our fixed positions. It is an unpleasant kind of work that often feels like torture to our habitual consciousness.

For this reason it is of the greatest importance when listening to dreams to stay away from snap interpretations ("I've got it!") and to listen to the dream with a willingness to bear the brunt of its utter incomprehensibility. Understanding a dream right away more often than not amounts to stringing the dream reality onto the chain of pre-existent conceptual forms. Thus it contributes more to a sclerosis of consciousness than to the actual self-unfolding of the image.

So now you are stuck with a dream that completely baffles you. That's a good beginning. Have the dream recounted to you twice.

Before listening to the dream for the first time, feel how you are in your body. Where are the energy blockages, where does it hurt, where does it feel good? Begin with your feet and move slowly upward. This gives you a chance to see whether your bodily sensations change during the dream recitation and in what way.

Then check briefly to see what is occupying you at the moment. What complexes are particularly active? This will give you the opportunity to see whether your moods change while you are listening to the dream.

Now the dream is recounted.

Listen with half an ear to the dream, and give the rest of

your attention to noticing where your mind wanders off to. At what point do you get bored, for example? At what point do you begin to think you're listening to complete drivel? You start to think about something that has no connection whatever with what you're hearing. Out of nowhere, an image from your past crops up that you haven't thought about for a long time.

Or you notice that the dream is unfolding against the background of a memory of your childhood buddy. In your world the action of the dream is taking place near your friend's front door. Or suddenly you get horny and begin to think about all kinds of pornographic images. An urge to masturbate might come up. Or you suddenly get angry. Or you get disgusted. And so forth.

For example, when listening to Stella's airplane dream, I was constantly thinking about a kid named Jimmy from my neighborhood in Holland. I see him walking along the canal. It has nothing to do with the dream. After the work on the dream is over, I make sure to recall this image again, as though it were my own dream corresponding with the dream that was just told to me. I suddenly recall that Jimmy died of the flu and that his last words were "Now I'm going to the angels." It was the first time anybody close to me had actually died. Obviously the dream constellated (aroused) primitive death fears and brought up the structural link in my world between death and *flying* angels. I must have unconsciously associated "airplane" and "sky" with "heaven" as the dwelling place of death.

I now have a relationship with Stella's dream *via my own image material*.

In short, when you are listening to someone else's dream

and an image of your own presents itself, one that clearly has no direct connection with the dream, let that image sink in briefly and see whether an underlying parallel to the dream develops out of it.

If a whole series of this kind of irrelevant images surfaces, make a random test with an image that strikes you as either very important or very unimportant.

When you've noticed that a particular part of the dream was very boring or nearly put you to sleep, take it as a rule of thumb that resistances are present in connection with that part of the dream. Resistances on the part of the dreamer are frequently unconscious and can be transferred unconsciously to the listener. Sometimes it is quite significant if, while listening to a dream, you actually fall asleep. Let the drowsiness come over you, and notice at what point you have become sleepy. Or perhaps in listening to the dream you got a twinge of pain in the knee. Before the dream you had a stomach ache, but then the knee was doing fine. You concentrate on your knee and feel how you're holding back a kick. You want to kick the dreamer. Why? You don't experience any conscious aggression. Then you notice that you always feel a similar need to kick someone (yourself included) who is trying to pull the wool over your eyes.

Suppose you got a pain in your lungs. Taking a closer look, you realize that while listening to the dream you were holding your breath, and the whole dream atmosphere gave you the feeling of being shut up in a tiny closet. (Every dream has its own atmosphere, just like the heavenly bodies. Often such an atmosphere is the only thing that is left behind from a dream.) Or you have an itch on your scalp. Your head is irritated. The intellect is exposed to little irritations. Metaphors often present themselves as literal symptoms in your body.

Instruct the dreamer to tell the dream as much as possible from inside; that is, as though the dream were taking place right now. In that way the dreamer can evoke the details and atmosphere of the images in his or her mind in the clearest possible way. Ask the dreamer to be a kind of a tour guide showing travel companions around in the dream.

Now the dream is told for the second time.

By now a process has already taken place. The first telling is reflected in the second. Connections pop into view. You listen to the dream images and try now to keep your attention fully on them. You listen to the rhythm in which the dream is told. Where does it go faster? Where does the tempo begin to drag? You listen to the intonations, heeding expressions of body and face. In short, you observe the dreamer as he or she tells the dream. I also often close my eyes while listening to dreams and concentrate mainly on the voice. This is very much an individual matter. Try to visualize the images along with the dreamer. For example, in the airplane dream, you note that an up-in-the-air/down-to-earth theme is involved. You try to observe whether there is a specified standpoint from which you are looking at the dream. For example, I see this dream from the standpoint of the Doctor in White.

At this point it is advantageous to have the dream in written form in front of you so you can also follow the dream as a text. There are dreamworkers who are opposed to recording dreams in writing because writing dreams down reduces their reality to that of a fixed text. This is a good point. It is important to let the dream speak, without allowing the dreamer to look at the written text. In this way the dream can be told from within the remembered dream imagery. It is also interesting to observe where the first telling deviates from the second.

Now you begin to analyze the text.

At this point you might throw up your hands in despair and say, "I can't cope with all this at the same time." In that case, let me give you a hint: Forget all the remarks I've made until now. They're just a few rules of thumb that sometimes help, a bit of advice for developing the discipline of dream craft. In this work it is important to learn things and then forget them again so as not to hamper the faculty of spontaneous observation, through which you can discover your own strengths in working with dreams.

Often your greatest strength in working with dreams is a trait that you usually consider your most unattractive weakness. For example, you catch yourself being very suspicious. You always look for the worst in people—a habit of yours that you don't like very much. In working with a dream it is often useful to let this rotten trait emerge, because a rotten trait can often sniff out something rotten in the image material—aspects of the image where rottenness and an ugly stench prevail. In this way, your suspiciousness becomes an instrument for detecting negativity. Once you have discovered the rot, it is important to let go of the destructive value judgment that is part of suspiciousness. In this way you make use of the powers of observation inherent in suspicion and not its destructive judgment. Or maybe you have a hypersensitive gut that always gets knotted up when things are tense. This symptom may be the site of your hypersensitivity, your perceptivity. It is important to listen to the dream with this hypersensitivity. In the case of gut symptoms, listen with one ear to your belly, noticing when pain appears and what kind it is. The tension that you pick up through these symptoms might be related to an aggregation of emotion in the dream.

But in listening to dreams, it is of primary importance to take the approach that anything is possible and that our grasp of the dream world is about as advanced as a baboon's grasp of algebra.

So far, this chapter has been devoted to listening to other people's dreams, because working with the dreams of others is a lot easier than working with your own.

The most sensitive images are protected by a hedge of resistances that keeps the emotional force of the images away from your ordinary consciousness. This is a way of keeping at bay emotions that do not fit your habitual self-image. When habitual consciousness looks at a dream, it will try to adapt the image material to your so-called self-knowledge. A lot of repressed material will remain repressed, and significant images will disappear underwater. Even if you really *want* to work on dreams by yourself, you will run into this obstacle. Often, however, a thousand and one reasons occur to you for not working on your dreams today, especially after your first enthusiasm has waned. Thus it is important to work on dreams together with others. One or more other people supply an auxiliary consciousness that can see in areas where habitual consciousness is blind. The other people can see things you might overlook.

With their help, your habitual consciousness can stay with images that it would otherwise flee from in subtle ways.

There are two different ways to work with others on dreams outside of therapy: reciprocal work in pairs and work in dream groups.

In reciprocal work, two people regularly work together on their dreams. In my experience, it is useful for each of the partners to have his or her own turn. For example, it's your turn the first hour and mine the second; or we do your dreams on Wednesday and mine on Friday; or you work this week with me and I work next week with you. The advantage of having a fixed schedule like this is that the external tasks are clearly established (during a certain time it's my task to listen and yours to tell your dream). If the work proceeds like this over a *long period*, a dream memory develops in which images from new dreams and earlier ones can be linked. This is an advantage.

The problem with reciprocal dreamwork is that transference—unconscious role-playing—sometimes gets complicated. Therefore it is important to check regularly to see whether the dreamwork is falling into certain fixed patterns. For example, in working on your dreams I identify most of the time with the older authority figures, while you always identify with the child figures in my dreams. Or I always feel like the victim when I'm working on your dreams, and you feel maternal toward my dreams. Discuss regularly what kind of roles you've fallen into. If you get completely bogged down, recount the situation to a third person, whose job is only to listen.

Some people find it sensible to work only with people with whom they have no relationship other than this work on dreams. Considering that dreams often unconsciously pertain to sexual and power problems, it is better to have a relationship that is fairly simple, not complicated right from the start.

It is also desirable sometimes to limit dreamwork to an hour or so per week, so that the intimate images that may surface will not be a daily influence on the relationship of the two partners.

As for the work itself—and this goes for group work, too—*the dreamer should discover what the dream is about.* The job of the listener is only to bring close the images that the dreamer gives less emphasis to and to help the dreamer get involved with the images. It is not a matter of interpretation. The dream images must reveal themselves through the constant attention paid to them. The only job of the listener is to maintain this constant attention to certain images so that the dreamer does not fall prey to the resistances of the I-figure in the dream and does not run away from particular images. The listener also should respect the dreamer's desire not to go deeper into certain images. Both partners should feel secure and comfortable and determine their own limits.

Often the intimacy that develops in reciprocal work on dreams is too threatening, and the somewhat less concentrated format of the group becomes preferable. The advantage of the dream group is that a dream image bounces back at the dreamer by way of different listeners, so that more perspectives on it can appear. As long as nobody makes the assertion "This image means this," each person in the group can ask questions aroused by the image. It is everybody's task to keep the dreamer focused on the images. Everyone can then decide as a group which images of the dream should be worked on. Or a group leader can be appointed, either permanently or by rotation, who ultimately determines what direction the group takes with a given dream. Just as with reciprocal work, it is important to reflect upon the dynamic between the group members and to watch for the development of fixed roles.

For work on one's own dreams, I generally consider it helpful to conceive of the work as a dramatic event (see, for example, "Driving In" on page 1). Imagine that you are working on a dream with someone whose job is to keep you focused on the images and to ask you questions. If clear-cut opinions come up about the dream, then ask, "Who is saying that? Which inner voice is expressing this conviction?" The answer might be "This sounds like my mother/my father/my astronaut-side." In posing this question, you often find out that the I-figure in the dream is identified with a similar kind of voice. Getting free of this identification can help you to see the dream in another perspective. Otherwise every dream is seen from the standpoint of the habitual "I," which makes dreamwork extremely boring. Consider the following dream, for example:

> I'm standing by the window and see a woman being raped outside. I turn away and don't want to watch. Standing behind me is a woman who finds the events outside completely normal and not in the least bit shocking.

The first reaction of the dreamer on waking is: "That rape was so horrible—something in my life must be completely on the wrong track." With this reaction, she begins to work on the dream but gets no further than the feeling that something is going wrong in her life. This evokes a feeling of panic.

When she presents the dream to us in a dream group, it evokes a unanimous reaction from the group members: the dreamer must be protected. On closer examination we identify this reaction of the group as a maternal response to the dreamer, as though she were a small child and a victim. We are identifying with a mother who wants to protect her child from the big bad world out there. This identification blocks all further work on the dream. Only when we turn our attention to the woman standing in the background, who regards the rape as completely normal, can we make progress with the dream. The mother-child complex, which has swallowed up the dream, now cracks open, and it becomes clear that the dreamer is trying desperately to hold on to her innocence and naiveté. She creates an artificial world in which she can be sweet and gentle. At the same time, she experiences the world around her as cruel and malevolent. The dream points to the loss of her sweet virginity, the end of a one-sided self-image.

In her own work with the dream, the dreamer—like the group—identified with the protective mother who wants to avert her gaze from the evil of the outside world. As long as this identification is not recognized, no progress in working on the dream can be made, regardless of whether the dreamer works on the dream alone or with someone else.

Again and again an inner voice pipes up that can prove that you have done everything wrong and that this dream shows how stupid you've been yet again. Especially when you already feel wretched, the guilt feelings pile up. Keep asking,

"Who is saying that?" Also try to feel where in your dream you lose interest, where you nearly fall asleep, at what place you find yourself bored stiff. These are the points of resistance. It is the job of the inner partner in the work on dreams to bring you back to these points. The inner partner should say regularly, "Let's go back now to the dream image."

Just as in reciprocal dreamwork, you should sometimes check to see what kinds of specific figure the inner partner is developing into. You might find that the inner partner recently has been extremely accusatory or childlike, for instance. In that case you will approach all your dreams from the perspective of guilt or with a playful sense of innocence. Your work will become very one-track-minded.

Work on dreams is a dramatic activity in which many roles are played. This comes from the fact that the dream itself is a product of what used to be called the *theatrum psychicum*, the theater of the inner world. When all the characters are carefully imagined, the images are put under pressure, emotions heat up, and the dream is being cooked.

– 4 –

Returning to Dream Reality

A vital element in dream work is the return to the reality of the dream. The dreamer moves into the inner space of the dream to the extent that the images can be recalled. In this remembered dream space, the dream events reoccur. This is an essential component of dreamwork. In particular, fresh dreams that are retained as spatial dream images and survive as real events, not just as a story, must be approached as much as possible through their spatial details. Fresh dreams are usually those of the previous night or dreams that have left behind a particularly strong impression. Some dreams remain fresh for days.

The activity of entering the dream world by way of daytime consciousness is a discipline of the imagination. In contrast to passive daydreaming, during which images are merely perceived, in this disciplined imagination an active interaction with the image world takes place. The faculty of memory is actively used to reconstruct the dream reality, as we discussed in Chapter 1. After this reconstruction, which often begins with the vague remnants and ruins of a dream, it is possible to continue dreaming the dream. This art is called *active imagination*.

The following dream can serve as an illustration. The person in question is a stiff white professor in his middle years who came into analysis because of dependency, after prolonged psychiatric treatment, on a whole arsenal of medications. He dreams the following dream.

> I'm walking through a run-down black neighbor-hood. I'm right by the bridge that will take me to the white neighborhood. I don't feel completely at ease, although I'm not frightened. I stop near a tall young black man. He is hanging on the jungle gym in a playground. The bars are really too low for him, but he keeps his feet off the ground by swinging his legs around in a counterclockwise motion. His feet touch me. I move back. But the farther back I move, the farther he swings out. He keeps on touching me. I walk calmly away. He comes after me. I get angry at him and curse him out. I tell him that he has to leave me alone. He stays back but still throws a stone at me when I'm on the bridge. He doesn't hit me.

The dreamer's first reaction in telling the dream is an un-dertone of pride that he didn't run away from the young man but rather defended himself.

We go back to the dream, and he says that the young man is very limber. He describes the jungle gym and the surround-ing houses. It all makes quite a run-down impression. It be-comes clear how much the dreamer fears the black man. At the same time it appears that the young man wants to come in con-tact with him; he keeps trying to touch the I-figure. This irri-tates the professor immeasurably, and he gets angry. At this point I ask the dreamer to describe the whole dream environ-ment precisely. I also ask him what the young man looks like now. Then I ask the professor not to be so aggressive toward the man this time around. Now it comes out that the black man has no malicious intentions. What is frightening the dreamer is his own prejudice regarding blacks. This specific black man appears to be different from the way he is in the dreamer's prejudiced view. In dreams, just as in daily life, we frequently react to the figures we encounter from the standpoint of all kinds of prejudices. When reliving a dream, it can be useful to suspend this prejudice and let the dream figure speak for himself. I suggest to the professor that instead of the tirade he aimed at the young man, he should ask what he wants from the dreamer, why he keeps touching him. The dreamer does this. The young man answers immediately, spontaneously, "Don't be so uptight, man! Hang loose!" The black man starts to laugh. "Relax, man, relax. Don't be so tense."

This short dialogue brings out a characteristic of the young black man that was present in the image: he hangs loose. He is a relaxed figure with whom the terribly tense professor has little affinity. Through the dialogue, a relationship develops between the dream figure and daytime consciousness. It is now possible for the professor to consult the young black man from time to time when he feels particularly tense. At such moments, he can evoke the black neighborhood and have a further conversation with the young man. The stressed-out daytime consciousness can learn relaxation from this dream figure. This is not a relaxation imposed from the outside by medication but one that arises from within, out of an independent inner need. In the dream, habitual consciousness remained ultimately untouched by the relaxed young man ("He doesn't hit me"). The active imagination, however, does not let itself be carried away by the resistances that the stiff professor (the figure with whom the "I" identifies) has toward the relaxed man who hangs loose. Thus, the active imagination can establish contact between the dreamer and relaxation. This diminishes his identification with what makes him into a stressed-out, uptight person.

The concept of active imagination comes from C. G. Jung. He describes his discovery of active imagination in his autobiography:

> . . . I let myself drop. Suddenly it was as though the ground literally gave way beneath my feet, and I plunged down into dark depths. . . . But then, abruptly, . . . I landed on my feet in a soft, sticky mass. . . . I caught sight of figures, an old man with a white beard and a beautiful young girl. I summoned up my courage and approached them as though they were real people, and listened attentively to what they told me. . . .[1]

In an ordinary dream, the I-figure sees the other dream figures as ordinary people. The dream reality and the daytime reality are usually indistinguishable. In active imagination, your sense of reality is different from what it is in an ordinary dream. There is a continuous awareness that you are dealing with a reality distinct from daytime reality. That is why Jung says in his description that he "approached them *as though* they were real people."

In active imagination, you are aware of this difference in

the nature of the figures you encounter, yet at the same time you regard these different entities as *real*. They seem to be real beings who behave autonomously in the same way that dream figures behave entirely independently of the I-figure. Active imagination assumes that, just as in the dream world, many different bearers of consciousness exist simultaneously and that the I-figure can make (renewed) contact with these dream beings through disciplined active imagination.

It is advantageous to begin a process of active imagination with a dream image, because the sharpened memory of the dream reality can change naturally into active imagination. Take, for example, this dream told by a nurse:

> I'm on the night shift and have to make my rounds. The room where I find myself is brightly lit. First I go to Room 1. It's dark in the corridor. I go into the room. Here it is very dark. Vaguely I see an old woman standing with her back toward me near her bed. I switch on my flashlight. I see that she has a big black-and-blue mark on her neck.

We start our work on this dream with the nurse's room. The light is bright, almost glaring. The desk she is standing next to is white formica. It reflects the neonlike light. The room is rather small. The corridor has a grayish floor covering. The dreamer cannot clearly see where the light is coming from; it is rather dark. The door of Room 1 is bare wood. The doorknob is to the right and is silver-colored. Inside it is pitch dark. There is a hospital bed and a night stand, but nothing is clearly visible. Once the flashlight is on, the dreamer sees the old woman at a distance of about eight feet. The old woman is thin. She's wearing hospital pajamas. The nurse does not know the woman. From that distance she clearly sees the black-and-blue mark on the woman's neck. At this point the dream memory ends. The dream memory has led her to an image that feels very real.

Now the active imagination begins. The transition from dream memory to active imagination is hardly noticed by the dreamer. She begins to move toward the woman. The black-and-blue mark is now extremely clear. The old woman is still standing with her back toward the nurse. The nurse is now so close that she can touch the woman's neck, which she does. Then the old woman turns around. Her face expresses endless sorrow. The old woman and the nurse gaze at each other for a long time. They both stand without speaking and feel the sadness.

In doing active imagination it is important first to alter our state of awareness into an image consciousness. We can accomplish this through the very detailed recall of a dream image. Through this, the sense of reality of the image world intensifies and the I-figure can begin to move *through* the space of the image.

If you do not begin active imagination in such a state of consciousness, there is a chance that you will just fabricate stories, which produces a sense of unreality. In active imagination, you don't have the feeling of unreality; it is rather as if you participate in two equally true realities simultaneously: the world that is actively imagined *and* the world in which you know that you are involved in active imagination. By contrast, during the dream it feels as though you are participating in one reality, the dream world. Thus, active imagination is a state of mind that is distinct both from that of making up a story and that of the immediate dream experience.

The work on the nurse's dream shows how we pass from dream memory into active imagination and how the dream world itself creates new images spontaneously.

– 5 –

A Dream Series

Now that we have dealt with the texts of individual dreams, I am going to present a long dream series composed of eighteen dreams, most of them dreamed within a period of six months.

Dreams often group themselves around specific themes that begin to unfold over time. Images go through a continual process of change, and such a process can sometimes be followed in a series of images that have presented themselves to someone as dreams. The insight that emerges when we study a series of dreams is that dream figures are in a constant state of development. Like any living organism, they come into being and decay.

The following series is exceptional. Ordinarily I do not consider it a good idea to present exceptional dreams to demonstrate processes of depth psychology. Such examples arouse false expectations of dreamwork and create disappointment and discouragement, for only rarely do dreams present themselves with exemplary clarity. Usually, at first encounter, dreams are utterly impenetrable.

In the following dream series, creation and decay in the dream world are clearly portrayed. It is as though with the increasing development of the creative process, the destructive impulse is gaining strength at the same time. Because of the portrayal of this theme, I have deviated from my usual practice of not presenting exceptionally accessible material.

I will not give much personal information about the dreamer. Ginger is an artist getting on in years who came to me with a depression connected with the fact that late in her life she became alienated from her art. She had the feeling that something else had to happen before her death. She drowned out this depression with a flurry of activity, which exhausted her.

After two months of working with her on her dreams, it occurred to me that the theme of *mud* was coming up with a certain regularity. I began to follow this theme without making much mention of it in analysis. After mid-January, I sometimes said to her, "How about that, there's the mud again," but didn't go into it any further, since I didn't know why the image kept repeating itself. In connection with the dream of February 8, it suddenly became clear to me that the mud image was in a process of development.

Dream 1, October 2

Driving along a lonely narrow road. Long drive between narrow stone walls, 12 feet high, that had been blasted. Then an opening and many many men and horses working and some huge stumps of trees lying on the ground and the road no longer good for cars. . . . I started back down the road on foot; it was in muddy woods. . . . I was very very much on my own and frightened.

Dream 2, October 4

I drive down a very steep dirt road . . . it was quite scary. . . . Came to a very steep part and muddy. We got down all right. . . .

Dream 3, October 10

As we drove down . . . we passed two men in black top hats in an open black car. The engine was dead. . . . Lower down we passed the house where the party was. . . . Rooms packed with people in black. I got to the apartment. It was under repair. Four or so men fixing it. . . .

Dream 4, December 9

. . . I drove my car through this wild country; more and more tiny roads, then just a muddy footpath . . . I was lost—they directed me up a muddy hill, but it led nowhere. I was on foot and lucky to get back.

Dream 5, December 27

. . . There was a tremendous amount of light red *very* squishy mud or clay—it was all around the entrance to the back door, and one's feet got all stuck with it and it got into my shoes and you couldn't scrape it off. Just over the back door there was a rounded open hole. I was trying to fill it up with the mud. It all slipped through and down, but finally I got it filled up. Inside things were unfinished and medium-dark darkness. . . . Later we moved towards the front. There were traverses of heavy beams but between them was the same mud. I was standing on one of the beams. . . .

Dream 6, January 6

. . . The manure was used to best effect. . . .

Dream 7, January 6

. . . The workmen were still not finished with the construction. . . . I had to get a thin construction on the top of the wall. It was like a . . . fence . . . so narrow that it was very hard to get in and out of it. . . . I walked on top of a very rough stone wall. . . .

Dream 8, January 10

. . . Lots of large stones that they had dug up in making the back terrace were just pushed over to the side. But there was an excitement to all this change. . . .

Dream 9, January 19

We were in an open car. We had been designing a gate. . . .

Dream 10, January 29

It was a sort of subway entrance. A gateway and each side had to be designed. . . .

Dream 11, February 8

. . . He found this green vessel—sort of a teapot but without a spout—quite thick walls, the reddish clay showing at the edges. But where was the top? . . . We heard them coming back, the two Mafia-type men who had also been looking for the lid of the vessel. It was very old Chinese and worth a huge amount of money. They were coming quickly towards us. Would we be able to get the red door open in time before they got to us? . . . [The dream has two endings: yes and no.]

Dream 12, February 13

. . . Finally I made two little cabinets with doors and inside a ceramic tiled shelf. I used the tiles from the sample book. I also used some old tiles . . . near the two cabinets I put in a long, long mirror.

Dream 13, February 13

. . . A muddy box. The students were working on a big piece. They had to stand on the wooden edge of the box while working so as not to sink into the mud. One was already working. Another came. . . . We went over to the box and stepped right into the mud. . . . I told the student to stand up on the edge.

Looking up on a very dark tunnel with two tracks—the ceramic piece was coming out and we could begin to see it.

Dream 14, February 25

It was a question of building something at the corner of the fence on the sidewalk to close the opening. We had tried cardboard. It wasn't high enough and no good when it rained. Then one morning I saw the carpenters had built a wonderful fence out of new wood; higher than a person and strong boards . . . very very expensive.

Dream 15, March 10

It was a question of how to arrange the elements around the pentagon or octagon for the presentation . . . a record of different aspects of my personality. They were all large and small octagons and all the same ceramic texture. Chinese in feeling. With a raised geometric design. The raised part rougher in texture—the recessed part smooth. Very handsome the whole thing and classic in the Chinese manner—eternal as only the Chinese can be.

Dream 16, March 13

My aunt wearing a dress of black netlike material. It was very worn and where the cloth was thin, her pale skin showed through. I wanted to hide these places with black paint and started to do so. "Oh dear!" I said, "I'm afraid I put black paint on your arm." . . . "That's happened before," she said and continued. I never knew how hard it would be to drive a car.

Dream 17, March 26

A house under construction. A pit is where the cellar would be. A sinister man throws me into the black pit.

Dream in the Fall, September

I see a carrot grow. Orange-red. At the bottom of the carrot tiny new roots have grown. It is impossible but it is that way anyway. And the new tiny roots at the large carrot go deeper.

In the beginning of an analysis, often a dream appears that is a kind of prelude touching upon the themes that, symphonically interwoven, are going to constitute the material of the analysis. This does not mean that such a dream, also called an "initial dream," is prophetic. It is more like an overture to a piece of music into which all the melodies are woven in a short form. In the course of the piece, the themes are further elaborated.

An initial dream is not necessarily one dream. It can also be a cluster of dreams in the beginning phase of a process. Also, such a dream does not come about exclusively at the start of an analysis. An initial dream can precede any new phase in analysis. Like a briefly flashing precursor of dream life to come.

Ginger presented the first dream to me as part of our second session. The dream was the only one to come up between our first session, in which we made each other's acquaintance, and this second session.

The dreams in the series following dream 1 are given fragmentarily. The texts, verbatim from Ginger's written accounts, were selected from a total of about forty-five dreams from the period from October up to the end of March. The fragments were chosen on the basis of their inner connection with the themes intimated in the initial dream.

One image from the initial dream was of a painfully intimate kind and cannot be studied publicly. For the rest, the initial dream is complete.

The different themes in the initial dream are:
- car, driving
- lonely
- narrow
- stone
- walls, side
- high, downward
- explode, blow up
- open place where men are doing construction work
- horses
- tree trunks
- road impassable by cars; on foot
- mud
- forest

The central feelings are fear and loneliness.

As I said, the first image that struck me, especially after dream 5, was that of mud.

In dream 5, Ginger wrote *red mud or clay*. This gave me the impression that something was happening to the mud. Clay lends itself especially well to being formed. The first use of this mud/clay is for filling holes in walls (dream 5). This is of major importance, since the walls had been blown up (dream 1). There is a structured construction in progress (between the traverses, dream 5), in which tree stumps (dream 1), now in the form of beams, contain the process. The beams give the process form and keep the mud within bounds (dream 5: "There were traverses of heavy beams, but *between them* was the same mud").

Dream 11 speaks again of red clay. Now, however, the *red clay has been fired into an earthenware vessel*—a container whose opening must be closed with a lid. Making pottery is an act of culture that qualitatively alters clay. Natural *earth* and artificial *craft* are connected with each other. From that point on I was also on the alert for the image of earthenware to see what was going to happen with it. Before I said anything to Ginger about earthenware, the ceramic object at the end of dream 13 emerged from the darkness.

The car, the mechanism of movement through this dream world, no longer fits into (or suits) the road that now has to be traveled. A transfer takes place. Movement is now connected with feet. There is a shift from the external motor to transport by one's own power. This becomes clear in dream 3, in which the motor dies and is accompanied by a sort of funeral procession.

It is also mentioned what kind of car is borne to the grave—the open black car; a vehicle that is not closed. In the initial dream, the work is taking place in (or on) an opening, the opening in the forest. The first use of the mud/clay was closing the opening above the back door.

Dream 11 is about finding the lid to close the opening of the vessel. Dream 14 is also about closing an opening. I think the significance of closing the opening is connected with the stone walls that were blasted in such a way that the path was no longer contained.

A narrowing takes place (dream 1). In dream 4, the road narrows down to a footpath. Ginger is driven into the narrows; it is oppressively tight to the point where she has to muddle through on her own feet. The muddiness increases to such an extent that in dream 5 the mud and her shoes can no longer be separated. It's a dirty standpoint. Things are no longer smoothly freewheeling. It is as though the old structure has been blown up and a new (infra) structure has to be constructed.

The final closure of the new structure is of the greatest importance. Not only is the vessel in dream 11 very precious and of Chinese value (an eternity value, according to dream 15), but it also gives rise to the emergence of destructive underworld forces. This is the countermovement opposing the constructive force that is trying to close off the opening.

The narrow path leads downward. Decline. Muddling through. "I started back down the road on foot; it was in muddy woods" (dream 1); "down a very steep dirt road" (dream 2); "As we drove down . . . Lower down . . ." (dream 3).

The contrasting image is also given (in dream 4): "they directed me up a muddy hill, but it led nowhere."

The way up leads nowhere.

The way down leads through a gate into the world underground. "We had been designing a gate" (dream 9); "It was a sort of subway entrance. A gateway . . ." (dream 10).

The process that enters by the back door (dream 5) goes under the earth, underground. There is digging going on—in back: "that they had dug up . . . in . . . back" (dream 8).

Stones emerge in this construction. The stone walls had been blown up (dream 1). The constructive process goes by the way of the back. It moves toward the front (dream 5) and builds a gate toward the depths. An underworld of Mafia-type men contrasts with an underground world where earth turns to earthenware (dreams 11 and 13).

It also occurred to me that the image of *tree stumps* gradually changed: "traverses of heavy beams, but between them was the same mud" (dream 5).

Heavy beams are tree stumps that have been processed in a rough way. "A . . . fence" (dream 7): Wood is used for an enclosure. Craft transforms natural trees into an artifact.

"At the corner of the fence . . . to close the opening . . . the carpenters had built a wonderful fence out of new wood" (dream 14). The enclosure has to be closed up. New wood is being used. New wood is made of recently processed tree stumps.

". . . A big piece. . . . They had to stand on the wooden edge of the box . . ." (dream 13). Wood constitutes the box inside of which the work can take place. It can contain the mud. It is a new, containing *framework*.

"Finally I made two little wooden cabinets with doors" (dream 12). In a wooden cabinet something can be stored. A wooden cabinet with doors can be closed. In the dream the cabinet has ceramic tiles. Here the development of the wood and the development of the mud come together. A new frame of reference emerges: "near the two cabinets I put in a long long mirror" (dream 12). Once the construction of the wood and the mud into the two little closable cabinets with ceramic tiles has taken place, then there is also a mirror. The image of containment and mirroring—looking at oneself, reflection —go together here.

"Dark tunnel with two tracks ... ceramic piece ..." (dream 13). The process in darkness and obscurity takes place on two tracks. Two movements in opposite directions can take place at the same time, just as there are two cabinets, which can hold different contents. From one movement comes the earthenware. What is the other movement? Perhaps it is connected with the destructive force that already cropped up in connection with searching for the lid to the vessel made from red clay (dream 11).

A constructive movement like the one intimated in the initial dream has a destructive countermovement. This becomes particularly clear in the contrast between dream 15 and dreams 16 and 17.

In dream 15 the centripetal force reaches its high point. The centripetal force, centering, which is connected with earthenware ("the same ceramic texture"), is a manifestation of the *ordering* capability of the personality. All the aspects of the personality come together here around a midpoint, creating an image of great beauty and eternity. Immediately following this, in dream 16, the old woman with the pale skin appears in the worn-out dress of black material—the decay of matter.

Spiritual eternity is contrasted with material decay (dreams 15 and 16).

"I never knew how hard it would be to drive a car" (dream 16). It is hard to maneuver between these two forces.

In dream 17 comes the nadir of darkness: "A sinister man throws me into the black pit."

After dream 17, Ginger enters a long-lasting depression with a dearth of dream material. None of the themes treated above are touched upon in the dream fragments that she recalls. Despair that she will never again create a work of art alternates with the feeling of having done everything wrong in her life. Deep-rooted guilt feelings come to the surface. Then she falls and breaks a leg, which deprives her of freedom of movement for a long period. A month after the accident comes the dream about the orange-red carrot. It is an image of a large central carrot from which many new little roots are growing, attaining a greater depth than before.

A deepening and a differentiation have taken place at the root of her being.

Now there follows a period of great activity in which many art works are created. The first: a rendering of the large orange-red carrot that sprouted roots. Then come a number of life-size representations on the theme of the mirror. A reflective process has begun.

Through this whole dream series plays the alternation of conflicting tendencies: the creative process, in which a new frame of mind comes into being, versus the destructive process—images of decay, annihilation, and sinister figures. It looks very much as if the destructive development reaches its low point when the dreamer literally injures her body. The broken leg seems to be a perfect metaphor, portraying how all forward-moving development comes to a full stop in a moment of literal destruction. I have come across a number of dream series in which the constructive and destructive processes appear interwoven. It is as though a creative development goes together with a certain process of destruction and decay. Renewal is at the same time the dying out of the old.

– 6 –

Alchemy as Exercise

The foundation of our psychoanalytic tradition is Sigmund Freud's book *The Interpretation of Dreams*. In it Freud analyzes a few of his own dreams. The central dream, usually called "the dream of Irma's injection," was the first dream he subjected to an in-depth analysis. This dream forms the basis of his dream theory.

In this dream, a patient of Freud's, Irma, has become seriously ill. The doctors determine that her illness will be healed through *an attack of diarrhea that will eliminate the poison*. Thus our tradition of dream analysis begins in a filthy mess.

When Jung tumbled for the first time into the dark depths, he landed in a soft, sticky mass (see Chapter 4).

When Stella fell from the sky, she landed in a world of decayed slums with filth on the streets.

The stiff white professor found the one to set him free in a run-down black neighborhood.

Ginger began between blasted walls on a muddy downward path, getting her shoes dirty. Dream 6 says that the best use was made of manure.

A dark, often repugnant underworld is regularly the background of an incipient process of rot, rot that is necessary to permit a stagnated process to reach a state of dissolution. A period of stench, disintegration, repulsion, and depression is often our first acquaintance with the life going on in the background of the state we call "consciousness." Thus it is not astonishing that we try to make this dingy world accessible through the use of disinfected words like "the unconscious." This terminology is a dead giveaway of the profound desire of the foreground world not to have anything to do with the world of the background.

The background world enters Ginger through the back door. Freud, too, discovered the healing power of this world via the rear end of his own patient, his own sickness.

In the background of the soul a healing process very often takes place through dissolution of the elements that until that moment had appeared in the foreground as fixed structures of the soul's life. It is for that reason also that such a process of change makes one feel as if solid ground were being pulled out from under one's feet. The elements that until now had dominated the life of the soul rot away, making room for new developments. Such a process of decay is frightening; something is dying off. Dying and death come into the foreground.

If such a process takes place without any preparation, the fear of the destruction of the old consciousness can become so great that the development is blocked. Hence in Ginger's process a vessel was constructed, symbolizing the ability to contain the change that was taking place in her soul. In an analysis in which two people jointly get involved in dream material, there arises a certain measure of intimacy and trust, a love relationship that is sometimes called transference/countertransference. In analysis, all the forms of love (including hatred) that the dreamer has ever known or imagined can come up. The dreamer and the helper work together, and the relationship between the two must be such that it can contain the material that surfaces from the darkness. The relationship can be strong or less strong. There is a connection between the atmospheric pressure that can be put on a relationship without its collapsing, and the depth of that relationship. A relationship that can withstand great pressure can contain many explosive situations without going to pieces. The erotic pressure pervading a relationship in which all kinds of intimacies can be experienced may become very great.

We have described psychic processes with alchemical metaphors. We have spoken of filthy shit, darkness, depth, blackness, mud/earth, manure, rot, stench, dissolution, decay, dying and death, the container (the hermetic vessel), and all kinds of fantastically beautiful and clean, foul and kinky forms of love and fire.

These images are also prominent in the image world of alchemy. It struck psychoanalysts early on that there were connections between dream images and the images of alchemy. Following the work of Herbert Silberer, C. G. Jung turned to alchemy to learn about our world of dream images. As well as being the archaic form of chemistry, alchemy also comprised the study of processes of imagination that took place in connection with the impossible task of transforming base metals into precious metals. This unreachable goal of refining matter through technique, concentration, and God's help aroused the passion of many in medieval times.

During the fifteen hundred years in which alchemy was

practiced it became extremely elaborate. I will give as an example a description of three worlds of images that are described time after time in alchemy: the black world, the white world, and the red world. The reason I concentrate on those three image worlds is that through them a view of the world is presented that differs from familiar dualistic categories such as masculine and feminine (described in alchemy as king and queen).

The black image world is called the *nigredo*. Its metal is lead.

The weather conditions there are dark, eerie, creepy, frightening, putrid, depressive, and melancholy. This moment of depth brings contact with the underworldly, the inferior. This is a time of debasement and getting lost.

According to alchemy the nigredo is the initial phase of *every* process in which a transformation of form takes place. First, things must rot thoroughly like garbage, before they can be reduced to the rubble of disconnected parts in which the creative power once again has free play. The alchemist says that everything in the beginning is bitter and rotten. Initial processes either lead to putrefaction or have their beginning in rot.

In this state of nigredo, one feels as though the whole world is falling apart—and especially that this nigredo state will never pass away. The future is dark and confused. It seems as though the feeling of emptiness and isolation will last forever. The tempo of life in the midst of this rotting is sluggish. All energy drains out of consciousness. In this bottomless pit one finds death, death as the only reality.

The white world is called *albedo*. Its metal is silver.

The heavenly body of the dark night is the moon. The albedo is a moon consciousness, light cast in the darkness, the cool, reflecting light of the eye of night. It is not a sharply circumscribed world with clear forms, but a consciousness of imagination and adaptation to darkness. Mercury, god of thieves in the night, he who accompanies souls to the underworld, is at home here like a night wind by a full moon. Lunatic thoughts, ambiguous allusions. Mercury feels quite at his ease in the albedo and constantly inspires the imagination with his duplicitous tricks. Henry Corbin shows how the world of the imagination is a world of images in a mirror, without the actual mirror; a reflection.[2]

A possible relationship between the nigredo world and the albedo world is described by Jung: "The situation is now gradually illuminated as is a dark night by a rising moon. . . . This dawning light corresponds to the albedo, the moonlight."[3] Reflecting in a dawning consciousness of fluttering night moths, here everything that had been taken literally now becomes metaphor. It is a world of poets, thieves, lunatics, and figurative language; an intermediate realm between bright, clear daylight and pitch-black night; the mediumistic world where one thing can also be another.

A dubious ambiguous existence in which you are drawn from one doubt to the next.

The red world is called the *rubedo*. The rubedo metal is gold, the congealed fire of the sun.

The heat of sunlight, the central source of life, begetter of all force, has taken on a solid form. Gold, says the alchemist, is the seed of the sun, while silver is the seed of the moon. In the sun world conflicting passions ignite enthusiasm through continuous friction. The sun brings development to all forms that lie hidden in the womb of the earth.

Under the sun everything is bright and distinct. The sun rules over order and clear perception. The world of the rubedo is also that of the bond between masculine and feminine. All forms of relationship between the two sexes find their expression here; it is a world of libido. (Recall the orange-red carrot of Ginger's dream.) It is a world of conflict and clash, of fusion and marriage.

According to Jung, "The alchemists term this the rubedo, in which the marriage of the red man and the white woman, sol and luna, is consummated. Although the opposites flee from one another, they nevertheless strive for balance, since a state of conflict is too inimical to life to be endured indefinitely. They do this by wearing each other out; the one eats the other, like the two dragons or the other ravenous beasts of alchemical symbolism."[4] (Compare my Angie dream.)

The ruler of the rubedo is the mighty lion, which subjugates everything. (A shadow of it is visible in the power-hungry bulldog in the Angie dream.) The rubedo calls to action—decisive, willful action, focus and discipline. It evokes a heroic world of highly visible, warlike feats. Whereas in the nigredo a nadir is reached, here the sun climbs to its zenith. Heat increases, and at the melting point the conflicting elements fuse into a new alloy, a new quality; it is a fusion of dissimilar nuclei. Considering that heat at this point is a primary aspect of the process, the pressure and strain brought to bear on the vessel in which the process is taking place are great. It now becomes, as it were, a pressure cooker. The danger here is that the vessel might burst because it can't bear the strain. This would be a great misfortune, since in that case everything would have to start all over again at the beginning. A process blown to smithereens returns to nigredo. This can happen, for example, when love overheats and invites passionate actions that the existing relationship—the vessel in which the love is melted down—cannot sustain, and the relationship bursts apart. One way of letting steam out of the pressure cooker is *acting out*. Here, the nocturnal image world and the daytime world are confused with each other to the point that one's action is based on the projection of inner images onto the outer world. In this way the inner images can cool off, but the damage in the outer world can be great. For example, if I refuse to feel my own rage, I might project it onto you. I act out by viciously attacking you, because it feels to me as if you are furious with me, instead of the other way around. This will cool my rage but might destroy you.

The difficult process of the successful rubedo is that of bringing together and keeping together the experiences of what we perceive as inner and outer worlds. It is a matter of action that gives the tendencies of the image world their due and at the same time perceives the images in the so-called outer world and reacts to them. One then lives in a world of inspiration in which the sharp distinction between inner and outer, contemplation and action, has been diminished. Active imagination and imaginative action fuse.

EXERCISE 10
Exploring Three Worlds of Imagery

In the following sections I suggest words and phrases associated with the black, white, and red worlds. The words are derived from dreams and from alchemical imagery. The exercise consists in trying to call up an image in your mind for each word.

The words themselves are evocations of each of the three worlds. This does *not* mean that the image portraying a word is a *symbol* for one of the worlds. Thus the word *darkness* does not "mean" the nigredo; rather, darkness can call up a quality of the nigredo world.

Use the following words to evoke images.

Example. Two nigredo words given below are *desolation* and *wasteland*.

Imagine that you are in the desert, completely alone. You are here not because you want to be, but because you are the sole survivor of a shipwreck that made you end up in this desert. There is no sign of people, animals, or water. Imagine yourself in this situation.

This lost situation probably corresponds to moods that are familiar to you from your own life. These are nigredo moods. Repeat this exercise with each word that strikes you for one reason or another.

Example. For the albedo, words like *frog*, *skating*, and *ice* are given. You could imagine that you are skating on a mirror-like ice surface. Feel the way you maintain your balance and how slippery the ice is. Look at the slippery surface under you, in which you see your own image reflected. It is cold around you. There is snow on the fields. White. There sits a frog, maybe a bit numb in this cold landscape. The frog goes into the water through a hole in the ice. The frog feels equally comfortable on land and in water. Feel the difference between the solid ground and the flowing water. Solid and fluid. The frog lives in both states. Now feel what kind of mood you've gotten into: reflective, maintaining your precarious balance on slippery ice, solid and fluid at the same time, cold-blooded. Compare this mood with moments in your life.

The Nigredo

In the initial stage of the alchemical process, matter goes through a dark phase; the darkness of despair. In this realm there is no light, no possibility for reflection. The metal is lead, the heart is heavy, and in the lowest state of the nigredo there are no images. Pitch dark. This is the background for many images at the start of a process of disintegration. A state of decomposition, which bears within it the feeling of depression and melancholy.

In alchemy and dreams, the following images come up which express the nigredo; stinking water coming up from beneath, the stench of graves; plummeting into the depths, sinking into a well; heavy, irreversibly downward movements; humiliations, collapsing buildings, ruins, and burned-out rubble heaps; dung heaps and excrement, gnawed bones and skeletons, the aftermath of war, a climate of despair, Good Friday, the low point of the night of crucifixion. Desolation and wasteland; petrified, lifeless landscapes; torture instruments; and dying of loved ones, elders, relatives. The theft of large amounts of money; wounded animals; amputations. Chaos, confusion, the wriggling of vermin. Because of this, the nigredo phase can be a state of *massa confusa* (confused matter). Divorce, losing one's job, getting sick. The animals connected with this world are mostly dark and sinister: ravens, crows, eerie black dogs and cats (with a witchlike character), venomous snakes, rats, bats, sharks, squid, jellyfish, and bloodsuckers. In technological imagery: submarines, bombs, sometimes vacuum cleaners (which suck all energy away), handcuffs, machine saws for cutting down trees, steamrollers, sewers, gutters, hearses and other vehicles. In terms of human figures: Nazis and other sinister foes, jail wardens, hated racial groups, rapists, persecutors, and quacks.

In this world of nadirs, cynical and sarcastic figures often appear, derisive remarks are made, and the view is obstructed. Sadomasochism, repugnant pornography. Gloomy etchings and lead pencil drawings. In the nigredo, the process has freed itself of the fixation in which it was long bogged down. In alchemy, the mortification, the dying of the old king, the grandfather, takes place. Outlived forms that have ruled us for too long rot away now, so that a solution can be found, and stuck psychic material can disintegrate into its component parts. The old scenario no longer works.

The function of the nigredo is to darken all light so that the eye can become accustomed to the dark world. All complexes that until now were under the control of the central consciousness break down. Sometimes at this point the image appears of a many-starred heaven with no fixed reference points.

Consciousness loses its grip on the world and unconscious images stream in.

The Albedo

When the eye becomes accustomed to the darkness, when the blackness of night has been suffered through, the white light of the moon emerges. The light of the moon is reflected light; it creates a world of imagination that is at home in the dark. The metal is silver. It is a world of echoes, sounds, and voices, helpful voices as well as lunatic convictions and instructions.

Reflective surfaces of water, mirrors, laundry, washing machines, and all kinds of cleaning agents, soap (the albedo is often also called the *ablutio*, the whitewashing after the nigredo). Poems, letters, and anything to do with nonrational language belongs to the albedo atmosphere. Neon lights (cold light), ice and snow landscapes. Drifting without direction, falling over backward, walking backward, crabs. Voyeurism and fantastic eroticism. Glasses, basins, receptacles that you can put something in. Passive hanging around, daydreaming, taking consciousness-altering drugs (not stimulants such as coffee). Transvestites, transsexuals, sex changes. Pregnancy, incubation, and eggs. Pearls, crystals, and glasswork. Pale faces, bodies, and plants. Convalescents and illnesses in the process of healing.

The moods are pensive, full of fantasy, not tinged with strong emotion, cool. To this world belong night birds and moths, owls and butterflies. Low-flying birds and all kinds of white animals such as mice, sheep, polar bears. Animals that get along well in the night—foxes, weasels. Amphibians such as frogs and salamanders. Snakes that shed their skin and other creatures that molt. Beings that change shape. In terms of technology: skates, anything to do with the media: radio, television, film, pictorial arts. Vehicles with unsteady balance (for example, bicycles). Refrigerators, freezers, silverware, medical instruments, water faucets, water pipes. Further associated with the albedo are invalids needing help and people in the helping professions such as nurses, insane people who are not in a state of psychotic panic, psychopaths, esthetes, pale people, vain people, artists, clowns. Watercolor art. Salt, bitterness, and disappointment.

Everything is changeable. It is a world of gypsies, nomads, and soothsayers. The mood is introverted. There is no central, cerebral, ordering consciousness willfully asserting itself. Instead there is an attitude that tolerates the state of disintegration and is at home with dissociation. In this albedo a reflective patchwork-quilt consciousness returns to a world of darkness.

The white of the albedo must be distinguished from virginal white, the white of milk and ice cream, the white that stands for untainted purity. That is a pre-nigredo white, a creamy complacency with the clarity that exists before all doubt. Often the nigredo process begins with a burglary or rape that violates and sours the creamy, rosy initial state. The white of the albedo comes after the torment of the nigredo.

The Rubedo

First light, dawn. Sunrise. Gold and gilt, the tinsel as well as the valuable. Here enters the faculty of valuation, which ascribes worth and meaning, structures hierarchies, sees things as heated oppositions. This is the outwardly directed force of the central will. This value-seeking and value-creating consciousness constitutes the path of law. The right side in contradistinction to the left side (which is connected with the sinister, the dark, the irrational). Reason and measure. Standards and validity. Revaluation and currency. Ascending, growing crops, green abundance. Summer and lion. High points, peaks, high mountains (whereas the albedo world often takes place in the valleys). Regulations, stoplights, orders. Power, power-hunger. Cutting through the knot. Blood, courage, endurance. High-flying birds. Birds of prey that spy their quarry from afar. Bright eyes, sharp sight. Telescopes, binoculars, and microscopes. Rockets; spaceships, as long as they are on course (as opposed to drifting satellites). Space suits, oxygen tanks. Computers, abacuses, windshield wipers (for clear vision). Diving boards, springy surfaces, an elevator going up. Scientists, slave drivers, oil sheiks. Fire, internal combustion engine, garbage incineration, gas tank, gas station, gas fireplace. Booming laughter. South and east (the nigredo is connected with the west, sunset, and death, the albedo with the cool north). Meat, particularly red meat. Dictators, tyrants. Volcanoes, pipes and smoking articles (but not consciousness-altering drugs). Coffee, sugar, stimulants, vitamin pills. Physical exercises done for health reasons. Fast transport, schools, educational institutions. Soldiers, horses, horsepower. Manic states, extremely tall people, athletes. Knives, razor blades, pointed objects. Penis, carrot, red radish. Sugar beet, banana, tropical fruits, fructose. Spirits (if not drunk, as opposed to wine intoxication in the albedo), cosmetics (as opposed to face paint), skin, suntan lotion, suntan. Anything that reflects the essence of something. Blueprint, building plans. Oil paint. The center (as opposed to the periphery for the albedo). Marriage, marital problems. Relationships (sexual or not). This is the world of the ordering sun consciousness, valuating and active, extraverted and inflammable. Through inflammability and grasping for power, a situation can develop that leads to the nigredo; burnout, decadence, decline of power. Corruption, rot.

Such is the constant recycling of alchemical images. These alchemical exercises underscore a central principle in dreamwork: that *the training of the imagination is a discipline*, just as important as the training of the mind.

-7-

Maggie in San Francisco

In my dream *practicum*, we usually work on participants' dreams which we use as *practice* material to graphically demonstrate ways of working with dreams. You are hereby invited to attend a few of these dream practica.

It is a small room. The seventeen people have to sit rather crammed together, and the room reeks of paint. I sit in the corner, having a moment to pop an egg roll into my mouth before the clock sternly tells me that it's seven-thirty and time for my dream class to begin. I've worked the whole day and I feel the aversion and repugnance that always come up in me when I publicly work on dreams, because with dreams you never know. With most dreams, you get the feeling there's nothing you can do, and yet you've got to do something.

Fortunately, these people have been working on dreams for years. This group is not yet running smoothly, however, since we've only seen each other on two previous evenings. This is going to be the third meeting. Those who are a bit freer with their dreams had presented them in the beginning, so I had plenty of material then. But now I'm not sure if we're going to fall down a hole and no one will want to work on a dream. I'll be stuck with no teaching material. Then I realize that I'm *always* scared that there won't be any dreams, yet there has never been a time when I got stuck without dreams. I know that I'm afraid. For me that means I'm preparing myself for the work on dreams. Somewhere deep inside me I hope every time that there won't be any dreams and I can simply go home.

Fortunately, Maggie helps me out. She has "half a sliver of a dream" that she wants to work on. She is a small, plucky woman wearing a thick green mohair sweater. She has short dark hair and a quick eye that takes in situations rapidly. While her mouth is laughing, her eyes remain a little sad. We get along well together.

First, I ask the participants to look inside themselves briefly to take stock of their inventory. How do your feet feel? Your legs? A little pain in the knees. Take another look. Your stomach, your heart, your arms, your neck. What kind of mood pervades you? Are you feeling cranky? Are you mainly thinking about your spouse, with whom you just had a fight? Or do you feel just dandy? Do you feel light or do you feel heavy? Can you breathe easily? Do you feel your heart? Is it going fast, slow, rhythmically—how? The purpose of this introspection is to know what's going on inside yourself, at least a little bit, so that you can detect changes while listening to a dream. A dream brings a certain atmosphere with it, just as there is a certain atmosphere in a room you enter. A smoky room full of gangsters is pervaded by an atmosphere different from that of an old ladies' tea party. When you go into a house, you quickly sense the atmosphere. Your mood changes somewhat. In the case of the gangsters you get frightened and excited; in the case of the tea party you get bored, or vice versa. We notice environ-

mental atmosphere in terms of mood change. Now you know
what your mood is. This serves as a base line.

For starters, I have us look inward for a minute or two,
which also tunes the mood in the room to the inner world and
makes it feel more intimate. Then I have the dream told twice.
First, I urge Maggie to tell us the dream in the present tense,
not just as a story, but as a direct recollection of the dream images. I ask her to try to function as a tour guide in her dream
world, which means that she also has to be as graphic and pre-
cise as possible.

She closes her eyes and concentrates. Most of the listen-
ers also sit with their eyes closed, occasionally glancing at
Maggie. She begins. As if by themselves, my eyes also close.
Maggie says:

> I'm in San Francisco visiting with relatives that I
> only know in this dream. We're in a square. I'm
> standing a few yards away from them, busy taking
> pictures of them. Of the little group, I can see a small
> boy. His father is standing next to him. The other
> family members I can't see so well at the moment.
> My attention is definitely focused on the little boy. I
> have two cameras around my neck. On both cam-
> eras I have a few shots left. The film is almost used
> up and I want a few more pictures of the family. In
> the background is a building of pink and gray stone,
> granite blocks. Very solid. It is apparently important
> for me to take the pictures before the film is gone.

That's all I remember. It's not very much. But it stays with me.

At the beginning of the meeting I had asked for short dreams, because long dreams are much harder to deal with and I now want us to concentrate on individual images. I ask what the first reactions to the dream are. One man finds that Maggie does not seem very attached to the images. Another person felt a certain sadness in hearing about "the last pictures on the roll"—as if something was over. "Yes," says a woman, "it felt just like it felt when my family left home. The children out of the house, my husband gone. It felt a little like those last few days." Evidently a number of the listeners had a feeling in hearing the dream that it involved things winding down. Something coming to an end. I remark that it is important to stay close to this feeling while working on this image, all the more so because of the prevailing impression that Maggie is not very connected with the feeling tone of the image. The atmosphere was transferred to the listeners. It often happens that the more the dreamer represses feelings belonging to the dream, the more another person working on the dream with the dreamer can feel these repressed emotions.

The woman who feels just as she felt when her whole family left her may be experiencing the underlying mood of the dream *in her own image material*. In answer to my question she replies that this experience is no longer very fresh and that she does not think about it often.

Another woman is bored stiff by the dream. I point out that this could have to do with Maggie's unconscious resistance toward the dream. The feeling of the bored listener might be connected with the remark of the man who said at the beginning that Maggie seemed to be not very attached to the dream. In dreamwork it is of great importance to be aware of fluctuations of attention. Unconscious resistances often express themselves as boredom, fatigue, or a wandering mind.

A man says that in listening to Maggie he feels all his aversion to family visits come up. He adds that he doesn't think this has anything to do with Maggie. I reply that if he is to work with Maggie on the dream, it is important in any case to consciously experience this resistance to family visits and at some point to ask Maggie if she feels something similar. Even if it has nothing to do with Maggie, it is relevant to know how you are tuned as a receiver. In that case, you actually are involved in two dreams, your own and the dreamer's.

Now I ask Maggie to recount the dream once more. This time the listeners listen not so much to their own reactions as to the details of the image world that Maggie presents. An added advantage of having the dream told twice is that the second telling is mirrored in the first.

Maggie says:

> I'm in San Francisco. I don't know how I got there. If I'm there on vacation or what. I'm in San Francisco. I'm with relatives. Relatives I don't know. I have a cousin on the West Coast. But it's not her. No, I don't know these people. We're standing on the square. It looks like the center of San Francisco. We're standing somewhere in front of a building.

Yes, it's a large building. I see big granite blocks that make up the building. They are gray and pink. The building has a pointed roof—like this. [She makes a triangle with her hands to show what the pointed roof looks like. It is now clear that she is observing the image directly, from inside. The feeling that she is not fully inside her dream has vanished completely.] There are people going into the building in the background. It looks a little like a city hall. Or more like a building where people go to solve all kinds of problems. There might be a small claims court in such a building. Or the Department of Social Services. The building is beautiful but very heavy and serious. We're standing in a paved square. The little boy has shorts on and he has light-colored hair. His father next to him is dark blond. I know them fairly well. At least in the dream. At this moment I have no idea who they are. [We feel her distance herself from the dream for an instant.] No, I don't recognize them. I'm standing with these two cameras around my neck. I focus on the little boy, and I also want to get the building behind them in focus at the same time. I want to get the little boy and the big building in focus at the same time. [She pauses for a moment.] That was it.

Now I ask what struck the listeners about the images.

"She has two cameras," somebody says. "She has to concentrate on two things at once."

"This time I didn't find the dream boring at all," remarks the woman who had been bored stiff at the first hearing.

"I would like to know more about that building," somebody says.

"Yes, and about the relatives."

"And San Francisco."

The craving for associations is spontaneously coming to the surface. You hear the images and you begin to wonder about things you would really like to hear more about from the dreamer in order to be able to imagine the specific context.

"What else struck you?" I ask.

A woman says, "I don't know what this has to do with anything, but I noticed a pun. Two rolls. I'm wondering if there are two roles in Maggie's life in connection with her family. But I don't know how to ask that. It could take us far away from the dream."

A play on words like this is often a good lead to follow, but it is of strategic importance to concentrate on the reality of the dream images first. Otherwise the association could lead us away from the dream itself into all the complexes that are tangential to the dream. I point out the difference between Freudian free association—a process that tumbles from one association to the next—and Jung's active imagination, which sticks to the image and tries to enter it. Both methods are valuable, but it's a question of timing. In working on the dream, I will indicate at which moments I think such a lateral move into chains of associations could be fruitful.

I suggest that now is the time to go ahead and ask for associations, images spontaneously emerging in the dream while concentrating on the different dream elements. This is not a free association. The associations remain directly bound to the dream elements; they are associative reactions.

So we want to hear more about the building in the background, the relatives, and San Francisco. "And about photography," somebody suggests.

"Yes," says one man, "I've also got something I don't quite know what to do with. For me, when I think about taking the last shots on a roll of film, I always have the feeling: let's hurry and take the pictures so we can get the film developed. That seems very important to me, but I don't know how it is for Maggie."

I find this an excellent reaction. It's crucial whether the emphasis is on the last pictures or on the impending development. For that reason I suggest he ask Maggie about it. She replies that she is also very familiar with that feeling when she's taking pictures, but that actually in the dream the idea really is to take pictures of the little boy, the family, and the building before the film runs out.

Since we are now talking about photography anyway, I ask Maggie for images that spontaneously occur to her upon hearing the word *photography*.

"I have a camera. And I do take pictures. It's not an actual hobby. That's why I'm glad that the cameras in the dream are easy to use. Because I want to be sure that the pictures come out well. With those cameras I feel sure of myself."

I softly but audibly repeat the words "sure of myself" a few times, so that they take on a certain echo. When you pick out key words in this way, they become mood images or examples of a certain state of feeling.

Three voices at the same time want to hear more about San Francisco.

The way you ask a question is significant, since the answer depends partly on the question asked. Often it is a good rule of thumb to start with a general question and then move toward specifics.

In the case of San Francisco, I'd ask first, "What comes to mind when you think of San Francisco?"

And then: "Where are we in the city? Does that square in San Francisco remind you of anything?"

"I've never been to San Francisco," she answers to the first question, "though I have been invited to go and see my cousin who lives there."

At this moment a lateral move toward the cousin is possible, toward associations that lead away from the dream image. Who is this cousin, what kind of memories does Maggie have of her from the past, recently, and so forth?

"My cousin is not part of the family I want to photograph. At this moment I really don't know any of them."

"Your dream family," I suggest.

"The square is in the center of San Francisco," she answers to the second question. "We are in the heart of the city."

"The *heart* of the city," I repeat, "the center."

Now we have reached the point where we should get into the image more closely. Slowly I must start to put more heat on the dream image and to increase the intimacy between Maggie and myself.

"What do you see of the family?" I ask.

"It's pretty vague. I actually mainly see the little boy. The other members of the family are very shadowy. I know they're there, but I can't recall them."

In the memory, an automatic focus on the little boy has taken place. It is probable that at the time of the spontaneous dream the other members of the family were also visible, since a dream hardly differs from an everyday event. Yet memory has already selected out what it considers important—the little boy.

"What does the little boy look like?" I ask.

Her face now looks as if she's trying to get the image into focus. She's peering intensely at something with her eyes closed. She leans forward a little. Very alert.

"He has big innocent eyes and a mischievous mouth."

"What kind of clothes is he wearing?"

"Shorts and a sweater. Sandals."

"And the building in the background, what does that look like?"

"It's granite. Very serious and heavy. It's a public building."

"Public," I repeat.

"In the building, problems are solved."

"Problems solved; solution," I echo.

"It's a building where things are taken care of."

"Taking care of people with problems," I mumble, barely audibly, and thus with emphasis. Everybody is either sitting with eyes closed or looking at Maggie attentively. All these questions were aimed at pushing Maggie into the dream image, so that she experiences the dream from inside. Now seems to be the moment for a tiny therapeutic move.

"Can you look through the camera?"

She nods.

"Can you now focus the camera on the little boy and then on the building, then again on the boy, then again on the building? Can you do that for a little while?"

She nods and remains quiet for a moment. I can hear the clock ticking.

"The image is changing," she says. "The little boy is becoming very lively. He's starting to jump up and down. He wants me to give all my attention to him and not to the building."

"What's your feeling about that?" I ask.

"That's not what I want," she says firmly. "I want to get the little boy *and* the building in focus at the same time."

"What's the boy's mood?"

"He's happy. He looks carefree. Very spontaneous. A fun kid. Optimistic."

"And what's the mood of the building?"

"Serious and esthetic. Caring. Justice is administered there. Beautiful but very grave. Very solid."

At this point we could go in any direction. We could ask about the points in her life where such a light, childlike spontaneous mood arises that doesn't want to be disturbed by serious gravity. Where in her life does she have the feeling of having to take care of everyone, of having to make herself useful?

Both moods—the light, childlike one and the heavy, serious one—have to be explored, as well as the points in her life where those moods come into conflict with each other. We could examine how the two moods are in contrast and the points at which efforts are made to concentrate on both at the same time and where the childlike mood tries to prevent that by becoming very lively. Perhaps this image has to do on the one hand with Maggie's childlike optimism, which sees new possibilities everywhere, and on the other hand with her heavily weighing sense of responsibility, which may have an oppressive influence on her, resulting in guilt feelings at many happy moments in her life.

Since what I want to show is how the general forms in a dream become visible and how the dream structure fits together, I'm going to stop here. Dream structure is more or less impersonal. This dream could have been dreamed by anyone. Filling the structure with personal images requires a measure of intimacy that is not present in this group. The more personal the images, the greater the need for a closed relationship that can contain the emotions. The alchemists call this the hermetic vessel. When working on dreams in a group setting, it is of great importance to make an accurate assessment of how much intimacy a group can bear. The more personal the material that is brought into a group, the greater the cohesiveness of the group must be. Otherwise the dreamer soon feels that his or her very sensitive material is being exposed to a cold observing eye. In such a case, feelings of overwhelming shame can easily develop. Dreams can be worked on much more profoundly in a group where there is a cohesive bond of intimacy than in a group that is heaped together like loose sand.

–8–

Underwater

At the next practicum session following our work on Maggie's dream, I discussed the albedo in alchemy, because her dream had presented some images from the albedo atmosphere. An image often used by the alchemists in connection with the albedo is that of salt. Salt is derived from tears and sweat and is connected with nostalgia and bitterness. It was used by the alchemists as a kind of a fixative to preserve processes. They thought that without bitter salt, the oceans would dry up. Salt, it was believed, binds moisture to itself. Without salt everything evaporates. It works against volatility. Disappointment especially is a salt mine. Photography is a kind of salting of images to keep them from evaporating. Memory is fixated onto a film of silver, a light-sensitive emulsion that retains impressions, inside the *camera obscura*, the dark chamber. This evokes images of the reflecting moon in the night and of the silver mirror. Maggie had two cameras. Duplicity as well as ambiguity of impressions is related to the albedo and Mercury.

The practicum in which George presents his dream follows the session in which this discussion of alchemy took place. George lets us know right away that he's had a dream he wants to work on. He says that a dream image has been lingering this past week that he can't make anything of and that keeps returning. He seems tense. There is excitement in his voice, and it seems as though something is already forcing itself out of him, uninvited. Here is something that wants to be said; something wants to express itself. Michael also has a dream, but the tension you feel behind his voice and movements is noticeably less. Something seems to be happening with George. He is a scientist with a sensitive mouth and a short beard, and he is usually quiet. His eyes seem used to the microscope, his fingers to the keyboard of his computer at MIT. Now he has a poetic look in his eyes. I urge him to tell the dream from inside—a superfluous suggestion, since the image seems to surround him. His voice is now plainly quivering. I don't know if this has something to do with the dream or whether he's embarrassed in relation to himself and the group.

First, I have everybody feel what's happening inside him or her. One of the participants makes the following notes: "I feel my head buzzing. My knees feel wobbly. My feet hurt as though I've been standing up too long. At the same time I feel like I want to jump up. As if I'm on a borderline." After the dream is told, she notes that her earlobe now hurts and she feels as though something has happened in her back.

What these notes mean I don't know. I can cook something up about them, but the most important thing here is the sense of sharp self-observation bringing about an attention that is not just coming from the rational center.

Then George tells his dream:

I see a stainless steel bowl with water in it. There's a rabbit sitting in it. Its head is sticking up out of the water, and as I look at it more closely, its head goes

-87-

under water. I begin to worry about that rabbit and its health. But when I look at it, I realize that this is its natural habitat. That's the dream.

I look around and see that Francis, the movie actor, is laughing. He obviously finds the dream very comical. Everybody remains silent, and I look for a long time at Francis until he openly bursts out laughing and blurts out that the whole time he couldn't help thinking of a magician and how the magician conjures a wet rabbit out of his hat. He mimics the bafflement of the magician when he sees this dripping rabbit appear out of his hat. Everybody laughs. The tension is broken. Some of the others had a similar feeling.

George also laughs and points out that the strange thing is precisely that the rabbit is not wet at all. If he could take it out of the water, he imagines it would be dry. In fact, the rabbit's head was quite fluffy. It also looked quite fluffy under water. I point out that here we obviously have an extraordinary rabbit, a real dream rabbit. "Yes," George says. "That's why the image stuck with me so much. The rabbit does just fine under water. As though it were an amphibian and didn't get wet."

At this point I briefly explain the fallacy of naturalism. This false notion presupposes that the dream world and the natural world of daytime existence are identical or ought to be. For example: A rabbit belongs on land, therefore there's something fishy about a rabbit underwater. Or if in a dream we see a limping dog with festering wounds totter by, we immediately have the feeling that something is wrong in the sense that there's something that has to be improved.

The dream image itself, however, points to the dog's limping having reached a state of decomposition. Similarly, a bird that flies without wings is not necessarily a bird whose wings have been clipped. Perhaps it has always flown without wings, and this is just the specific quality of this bird. In short, a dream image does not have to be put on the procrustean bed of our naturalistic consciousness. In the nonphysical reality of the dream world, each monster has its own form. And that is what so astounds George—the rabbit is completely at home here. An underwater rabbit.

While I'm telling this, I become aware of an undertone of panic in my voice. I have no idea where to go with this dream. Now, this is my usual feeling. Generally I have no idea how to start on a dream. At such moments absolutely nothing comes to mind. Then a painful feeling of inferiority develops regarding the dream, and in this way my rational consciousness begins to sense its limits and my other faculties get their chance. Thus a wretched feeling at the beginning of work on a dream is completely normal. Other analysts also experience this feeling, as I have pointed out elsewhere.[5] Feelings of inferiority are closely connected with the work on dreams. But with this dream I've got a heavy dose of it, reinforced by a feeling of panic that seems to catapult me away from the dream. "I've no idea what to do with this dream," I say. "It's stainless steel to me."

My last sentence is an attempt to express my resistance in the language of the dream so that I can become aware that the resistance is connected with the dream and so the process of "metaphorizing" can be set in motion; making figures of speech out of literal words. Learning to see metaphorical forms in literal images is essential for dreamwork.

Jenny asks George if he can touch the basin. At the same time she makes a gesture with her hand as though she were pushing something away. I ask her to repeat the gesture. It looks like she's shoving something away from herself. I indicate to her that it is important to note such warding-off gestures so that one can sense what the resistance to the dream feels like. Clearly, others also feel the resistance to the dream that I feel. Jenny expresses the resistance with an unconscious gesture. I say that I also have a feeling of defeat and that I see working on this dream as hopeless. I add to this that it is important not to take this kind of feeling *literally*, because then you would drop all work on the dream at once. It is an atmosphere that seems to belong to the dream.

"What would happen if you pulled the rabbit out of the water?" someone asks. George thinks for a moment. "I believe the image would change," he says. "I think it would then become something like a sea anemone." People sit up straight. There's a shuffling of chairs. Attention intensifies. Clearly, it is easier for us to concentrate on a fantasy that leads away from the dream than on the actual dream image. Three different people want to know more about the sea anemone, and George is ready to tell them more about it. I interrupt him with the remark that we would be quite happy to get away from the image of the underwater rabbit in its stainless steel bowl but that it seems important to me first to go toward the image itself before we get ourselves into associative image chains.

The need to go to the next image seems to me to be a further indication that this dream is surrounded by powerful resistances.

Now we begin to discuss how to enter the image. Should we start with the rabbit, the bowl, or the water? Do we ask for associations, give amplifications? A heated discussion develops between advocates of beginning with the image of stainless steel and others who want to start immediately with the rabbit. I stay out of this and note that the atmosphere seems very cerebral. However, I don't say this, in order not to disturb the lively discussion. "Wait a minute," says George. "It's like the bowl is emptying out now. The water is running out of the bowl and the rabbit is getting very restless." I take this as a sign that we have to get out of this dry, cerebral atmosphere. But how? George holds his hand out. "What does your hand want?" I ask. He looks at this hand with surprise. He hadn't noticed that he'd made a particular motion with his hand. "Stroking," he then says. "I want to stroke the rabbit. It's scared." Now I know what has to be done. The course of action has been mapped. We must slowly approach the moment in which he comes into contact with the rabbit. Now we can begin.

A woman has a belated remark that she has to get off her chest. She's strongly reminded of *Alice in Wonderland*. It feels like a kind of magical event.

"First, let's look at the environment of the bowl. Is the bowl inside or outside, in a room or outdoors?"

I'm beginning by sharpening perception so as to return to the image without arousing a lot of resistances.

"In a room," George answers firmly. So he is definitely

back with the dream image and is speaking from direct observation.

"Can you see the ground? Is there a floor?"

"I see a ray of sunlight shining on the basin. I can't see the floor very well. Maybe wood."

"Can you see if it's wood," I ask sternly, "or do you think it's wood?"

"I'm assuming."

"Please don't guess!" It's a matter of sharpening direct observation. Guessing only obscures the actual image. "Where are you standing—or are you sitting or lying down?"

"I'm standing about three feet from the bowl, looking down on the bowl from above."

"And the bowl. Can you describe the bowl?"

"It's about two and a half feet in diameter, a foot and a half deep, almost filled to the brim with water. Flat bottom. It has a slight curve. Looks a little like a bath. There's a rim around the top of the bowl. The metal is silvery. I call it stainless steel, but I don't know for sure. It could be either. It is silvery, blue-tinted metal that has not been polished to a sheen. It has a gritty, rough metal surface, but you can see reflections in it."

I'm amazed at the precision of his powers of observation; he has clearly been trained in scientific observation skills.

"What do you feel about the bowl?"

"It feels almost a little cold," he says after a brief pause.

I see Jenny leaning forward. She says, "It feels just as if I could warm it up in my hands," and she makes her hands into a bowl. George smiles in agreement, his eyes still closed.

"It reminds me of the moon on the water of a lake," he

says. A lake, like the one in South America when he was on vacation, snorkeling underwater.

If at this point you want to follow the lateral movement of associations, you will get into questions about particular memories and associations connected with this personal memory. In this way you can penetrate the most intimate memories and images connected with that vacation and from there go into ever further reverberating associations leading to comparable atmospheres during other periods of his life. Then return to the dream image before you get lost in distant morasses.

"Let's come back to the bowl," I suggest.

He nods. "To begin with, it looks like something clinical, something related to a hospital."

"A hospital, a house full of sickness," I think to myself. A bowl full of sickness. A sick bowl.

"But it could quite easily take on another form. Then it becomes a silver chalice." I note everybody's attention is regenerated by the beautiful silver of the chalice. What a religious image! Everybody obviously feels it's beautiful. *Chalice* also means Eucharist cup. It's a little too beautiful for me. In this way it could easily become too exalted.

"Is there really a transformation into a chalice, or do you personally expect such a thing is going to happen?"

"I think it would become a chalice as soon as I touched the bowl."

"Touch the bowl then," I say as off-handedly as possible, in order not to arouse the resistances toward the bowl again. "Is the bowl changing?"

"It's changing a little. But not as much as I'd expected."

Now he's where he should be. Just like Jenny, he's now holding the bowl in his hands.

"Are you holding the bowl in your hands?" I ask in order to fixate the image a little.

He nods, attentively observing the image of himself with the bowl.

"How does that feel?"

"Heavy and alive at the same time," he says without hesitation.

"Where does the alive quality come from?" I ask. "From the bowl, from the water, from the rabbit, or from the whole image at once?"

"No," he says firmly, "it's all because of the connection I now have with the image."

Now that he feels the connection between himself and the image so clearly, I think it's time for a lateral move.

"What is that feeling like?" I ask. "You don't have to say it," I add carefully. "But is there a specific memory image that has just come up?"

He nods in some kind of trance. "The image is changing quite strongly now."

"Is it an emotional memory?" I ask.

He nods vigorously.

I say as an aside to the other participants that if we were now in an analytic, therapeutic situation, at this point George's emotional memory with all the associations following out of it would be investigated.

I ask George to concentrate on the emotional atmosphere

of the memory that we, the listeners, are ignorant of. I give him a minute. Then I say:

"Now return to the bowl. What does it look like now?"

"The water is lighter, sparkling, as though it were alive. It feels very good."

"Can you touch the water and feel the temperature?"

"It almost feels like body temperature." His voice has a questioning quality, as though he is expecting an interpretation from me.

"Does it feel like tap water, or salt water? How does it feel?"

"It has a high surface tension," he says, surprised. The more the observer is in a state of surprise, the clearer the distinction between his subjective expectations and the reality of the image he finds himself in. The image now has a large measure of autonomous reality.

"I can enter the water, but—"

"Wait a minute," I call out. "Can you stay with the moment where your hand is entering the water?"

He nods. "I have to exert myself. It's almost an electrically charged surface. I have to put pressure on my heart, it seems, in order to get through the surface tension."

The resistance has turned into the image of a high surface tension that is difficult to penetrate.

"What happens when you put pressure on your heart?"

"Warmth comes up. The water gets warm."

"Could you concentrate on your heart for a moment?" He does so for a few seconds. "My heart is filled with a great longing," he says. He sounds completely normal, not at all melodramatic or highfalutin.

"It's a great longing to be in the water."

"Are you familiar with such a great longing?" I ask casually.

"Yes," A memory image comes up.

"Can you feel yourself pervaded again for a moment by the emotional atmosphere of this memory image?" I again give him a minute.

His shoulders get somewhat rounded while he concentrates on the atmosphere of the image. Then he speaks.

"Now it's as if it aches. It all feels—the whole image feels—much heavier." The image has obviously grown weighty. I look around. The concentration in the room is now extremely intense.

"Is your hand still in the water?"

"Yes . . . or no. I had my hand in the water until you made me aware of it. Then it seemed to come out of the water by itself."

A deep sigh and laughter go through the room. The tension is broken.

"As soon as you think about.it, you come out of the water," I think aloud. "It's like the moment when the bowl emptied out, when we were talking about it cerebrally. But what I really want to get to is a question to everyone: Could you feel the change in depth when his hand came out of the water?"

Two-thirds of the listeners nod enthusiastically. Nobody denies having had such a feeling.

"Dreamwork," I say, "always makes me think of deep-sea diving, where you can clearly feel the pressure differences at various depths. While working on dreams, you can perceive change in depth in terms of *difference in pressure*. Atmospheric pressure."

"The water is much chillier now that I don't have my hand in it anymore." I choose for the moment not to get into this chilling; I just repeat: "Chillier when you're out of the water. As long as you're not thinking about it, you stay warm and inside," I say.

At this moment many lateral moves are possible (for example, "Do you know such moments of chilling?"). But I want to get to the rabbit. The attraction to the rabbit now increases noticeably in me. It is as though the rabbit were pulling me toward itself.

I give myself a moment to let this attraction work on me.

"Do you think we could get back into the image?" I ask George cautiously. He nods. As soon as we are again concentrating on the bowl, I feel how much depth we've lost since George's hand came out of the water. My attention is quickly distracted and nothing occurs to me. So I decide to start all over again. This slow process of repetition is aimed at raising the reality of images to a higher grade.

"How does the bowl look now?"

"It's whiter now. A bit like porcelain. Yes, it's now a white porcelain bowl on a pedestal."

"Oh," I say, "the bowl is now elevated; put on a pedestal, heightened?"

By casually injecting this play on words in the form of a question, a sort of disposable interpretation, the metaphorical quality of the image is brought to the fore. This makes a more explicit interpretation superfluous. The heightening of respect for the bowl is already clear in the figure of speech: "elevated; on a pedestal."

"Where are you standing?"

"I'm standing in front of the bowl. The bowl is at about chest height."

"At the level of your heart?"

He nods.

I make a mental note to myself that the bowl has gone through an albedo, a phase of whitening. Now it is white porcelain. So reflection has already exercised its influence on the image.

"Is there something in the bowl?"

"Yes, the rabbit is still there. It's moving in the water."

"How does it look?"

"It's white and brownish gray. Long ears. A twitching rabbit nose. It's jumping around a little underwater. Little rabbit jumps."

"What's the quality of the water?"

"As soon as you asked, it got a little darker, then lighter again. . . . A little like tap water, but somewhat bluer."

Now I feel the same level of depth as before. But every now and then, attention suddenly pops back to the surface. I am still slightly more aware of the city noises than I was before the break in depth. Before, I didn't hear the sirens of police cars and ambulances at all. So the depth quality is unstable. I want to stabilize it first by bringing him even closer to the rabbit.

"Can you get any closer to the rabbit?"

"Yes, I'm going closer to it now."

"What's happening?"

"It's changing. I can see the whole top surface. But now I feel more in my head, more cerebral."

That was what I was afraid of. At this point we are quite close to resistances that could easily keep us away from depth and profundity.

"Yes," I say, "I feel that too. What's happening to your heart at this moment?" Silence.

"That longing. But vaguely."

"Get into that longing. Let it grow."

Silence. His fingers are moving with a kind of unconscious grasping motion.

"Your hand still wants to get to the bowl?"

"Just to touch the surface of the water. I feel a strong resistance to going into the water."

Now he can feel the resistance. That means that he is no longer identified with the resistance, or is at least less identified than before. As long as you are identified with something, it's as though that is the atmosphere that permeates everything. It's so all-pervading that you can't actually feel it clearly.

The quality of depth now becomes more stable.

"How does the resistance feel?"

"My heart feels heavy."

Then, energetically, I say, "What happens with the rabbit when you stick your hand in the water?"

"The rabbit is scared. It gets bigger. Then later it goes back to its normal size."

Curious, I think that the rabbit gets bigger when it is frightened. Could that have something to do with the heart?

"How does your heart feel?" I ask out loud.

"My heart's beating fast."

I feel apprehensive about something that is about to happen and ask, "Are you apprehensive?"

He nods vigorously. "And how!" he says.

"Is your hand near the rabbit now?"

"Yeah, I'm touching it."

"How do you feel?"

"My heart is beating even faster now. I'm scared and full of expectation. . . ."

"What is the rabbit doing now?"

"It's putting its ears down. It's like it's giving me permission to pet its head."

"And are you doing it?"

"It's as if I have to stretch my arm real far."

"Is it nearly out of your reach?"

"Yes, it's like I have to push really hard."

Something is apparently being born here, I think, and I feel the increasing pressure on my heart.

"Do you have to push with your heart?"

"Yes, exactly. That's it. I have to put pressure on my heart. I have to use all my strength. Then I can only just touch it with my fingertips.

"How does it feel?"

"Soft and fluffy."

"What's happening with the rabbit?"

"It seems to be relaxing."

"How does your heart feel?"

"A bit calmer. It's beginning to relax. A freer feeling. The rabbit now feels like a pet. I can feel the bones in its head. And its ears. It's almost a dog. As if it were my pet."

Then he adds dreamily:

"As if I'd once known that rabbit . . ."

"What's the feeling of having once known the rabbit like?"

"It feels like in my earliest childhood."

At this point, in another setting, we would take a closer look at these images of earliest childhood that are now coming to the surface. These images seem to be closely related to the rabbit. The childlike heart.

We let him think for a moment about the images from early childhood.

"What is the emotional atmosphere of the early childhood memories?"

"Joy and fear at the same time."

"Let yourself be filled by those feelings."

I look around. The time on my alarm clock is almost up. Everybody's sitting with their eyes closed and feeling early childhood memories about beloved rabbit pets.

It's time. The evening is over and I'm tired. Just a few more minutes with the childhood memories and we'll come back to the room in which we're sitting as a group.

"Now we have to slowly leave the rabbit," I say, almost in a whisper.

"How does that feel, leaving the rabbit?"

"As I take my hand off the rabbit, it's as though I'm letting go of some part of my insides. Something that lives very deep down inside of me."

"How does the water look?"

"Now it looks like a mirror."

"Keep looking at the mirror."

In this *albedo* process—this whitening, this reflecting—a capacity for reflection has apparently developed that is connected with animated feelings from the magic of earliest childhood. A restored contact with the heart of childhood.

"Now we have to come back to the room," I say regretfully.

Dead silence in the room.

Slowly, eyes are opening.

"Thank you very much," I say, stowing the alarm clock, which had been on the little table next to me, in my briefcase.

"That was magical," a woman says to George.

He looks at her as though he were suspended between two worlds.

I go over to him and shake his hand. Our handshake is warm.

–9–

Movements through Space

From the work on George's dream it becomes clear that movements inside the dream image are of major importance, especially the movements of consciousness toward the dream figures and away from them. A specific emotional distance between habitual consciousness and the dream figure seems to be imagined as a physical distance between the two, a distance in feet and inches. It is a distance that sometimes must be bridged in order to get in touch with the dream figure.

Here are two examples of this.

Marianne is a small, timid-looking woman who for years worked with the Peace Corps in Asia and has recently returned. She dreams:

> A little gray mouse jumps out of my gray leather bag. He jumps onto the ground and runs through the room. From somewhere a cat comes running. At the back of the room the cat catches the mouse and eats it. I have a feeling of relief.

She presents the dream to the group with a brief excuse. It's only a tiny little nothing dream. She doesn't even know whether we can do anything with it. She is sincere in her conviction that the dream has little significance. It strikes nearly all the group members that she's telling the dream virtually without emotion. To check if she is perhaps afraid of mice, causing the sense of relief when the mouse was eaten by the cat, I ask her how she felt when the mouse came out of the bag. She says that she found the mouse very cute and adorable. She would gladly have caressed it, but the little mouse jumped away. At this point it becomes clear that consciousness reacts in a peculiar manner to the death of the adorable little mouse: according to her own account, she'd been relieved and apparently unmoved. By itself this doesn't mean that there is anything out of the ordinary going on, but her indifference surely deserves further investigation. Our work again begins with an image from which I intuit little resistance, the image of the bag and the little mouse. I try to keep easy interpretations of a sexual, pornographic nature at bay. She herself says that the images seem somewhat "Freudian" to her. Something about phallic mice in vaginal bags. We all giggle a little, from which it becomes obvious that the sexual has certainly been constellated. Nothing is as good an indicator of the presence of sex than the adolescent giggle. Nevertheless, I want to get to the murder of the mouse, the cute, adorable, little gray mouse. At this location I sense the greatest repression of emotion, the densest aggregation of vital force. In order to sharpen the memory of the image, I ask Marianne to describe the surroundings in which she finds herself when the mouse jumps out of the bag and begins to run through the room.

"I'm in the corner of a room. It looks a little bit like this room" (the room in which I'm teaching this dream practicum). As she describes the room in detail, it seems slightly different after all. A little deeper. Where the cat caught the mouse, it was rather dark. I ask her to focus on this dark scene of the cat pouncing on the mouse while at the same time remaining aware of her own location in the room. She again feels the same relief as during the dream. Actually there isn't much emotion at all. "I just see how the cat eats the mouse. It doesn't touch me that much."

She is standing in the room about twelve feet away from the event. I ask her to take a step forward. Now she says she is getting somewhat nervous. A little afraid. With the next step, the fear increases. I stop at this point to gauge how much more pressure I can exert. The emotional pressure here increases exponentially with each step closer to the dream event. It seems to me that she's pretty resilient and can take a bit more pressure. I ask her to take another step closer. She is now right in the vicinity of the mouse-eating cat. Suddenly Marianne begins to sob uncontrollably. We're all very quiet. I hope I haven't gone too far this time, particularly because she became this emotional so unexpectedly. Then she calms down some. Sobbing, she tells how she'd had a near-fatal accident that had caused her to go into a coma, hovering near death for months. Since then she had emotionally repressed the accident entirely. This is the first time that it has returned to the surface with its full impact. At this point she wants to end work on this dream. She says that even in her therapy (she's in analysis) she wouldn't have gone beyond this point. I tell her that she's right. Some swellings have to come to a head before they can be lanced.

In contrast to Marianne, Maria is very upset as she presents her dream at the next session. She had the dream two nights ago, and it put her under such pressure that she could

hardly wait for the dream practicum. She has a divinity degree
and wants to become a priest. She dreams:

> I'm walking along a long dark corridor. It's really
> pitch dark. It looks like a kind of very long tunnel. In
> front of me, I see light coming from a crack under a
> gigantic door. When I get closer to the door, the
> door swings open and in front of me is a blinding
> white light. It's so overwhelming that I wake up.

When we go back to the image and she is once more
walking through the pitch-dark corridor, Maria says that it
reminds her of a horrible time that is only barely behind her.
She's glad that she's moving toward the light again. When
she gets closer to the door, the white light coming from
under the crack lights up more of the space around her. But
she still can't make anything out. Then it strikes her that the
door is of heavy wood, without any ornamentation. When
she's some feet away from the door, it swings open. She says,
"The light is so horribly white. There are no forms in that
light. Behind the door there is only that light. Nothing else.
A sort of life after death. It frightens me and at the same time
it attracts me."

I ask her to approach the light slowly. When she's three
feet away from the door, she says: "I know for sure that if I stick
out my arm now, it will disappear. Everything disappears in that
white light."

Maria now begins to breathe noticeably faster. As, at my
urging, she goes and stands on the threshold, she begins to hy-
perventilate in a panic. Her breathing goes so fast that she

might well faint. First I ask her to breathe slowly and deeply. I myself automatically begin to breathe deeply. She becomes a bit calmer. Then I ask her what the white light feels like.

"If I go one step further, I'll disappear. Then I'll never be able to come back. It is very warm, but not terribly hot."

I ask her to feel the warmth in her body.

"It's strange. In front I'm warm and in the back it's cool. The darkness is cool. Actually it's a relief now that I'm standing in front of that white light." I suggest she feel the location in her body where the warm light and the dark coolness meet.

"A kind of line goes through my whole body. Down the middle of me lengthwise. It feels like it's red. The longer I concentrate on the line, the more it becomes a coiling red line. It's alive. It's just like a live red vein living between light and darkness." The longer I keep her with the image, the more her breathing is panicked. "That red being in the middle is coiling. I'm very scared. I want to stop."

I tell her to move slowly backward away from the white light and back into the darkness. "Walk slowly backward," I say. As she gets a little further back, the dread lessens. She begins to cry. The group is very still.

After a little while, Maria says, "The last thing I saw looked like a big pot of seething liquid. But I wanted to get away. I was so scared. I've never been so scared in my life."

The alchemists say that the human soul is stretched *between* the formless spirit of eternity and the darkness of the earthly nature. They call the human soul the *anima media natura*, the soul that partakes of both natures and that runs like a twisting coil between eternity and temporal existence. The alchemists were Christians whose Savior was crucified between vertical eternity and horizontal earthliness. In the Middle Ages the image of the soul twisting in pain between two worlds was still quite alive. The session stops at the seething source of torn vitality.

I step outside. The Charles River winds quietly between Boston and Cambridge.

– 10 –

Amplification

According to my standard Dutch dictionary, the word *amplification* means: "1. literally, enlargement; figuratively, a more ample exposition of a thought, proposition, or image; 2. exaggeration." As applied to dreamwork, as a term of the craft, it indicates the technical procedure that attempts to reinforce the image from outside by letting it resonate in an echo chamber. This echo chamber is comprised of images borrowed from collective consciousness, that is, from the common stock of images alive, in either recorded or unrecorded form, in the memory of mankind. This can range from television advertising to religious images, from pornographic pulp to Dostoyevsky. Anything that has ever been expressed by people can be used to color and deepen the specific tone of an image. Thus amplification is *not* primarily concerned with the *meaning* of images.

In amplification we ask the question: "What is this like?" It is a question about the physiognomy of each image. Each image has its own face, a face we have to face. Learning to see *resemblances* is, according to Aristotle, the beginning of all art in dream craft. In doing amplification—amplification is an activity, an *operatio*, to speak in alchemical terms—you let the dream image echo off commonly existent images that resemble it.

The woman at the session in which George presented his dream of the underwater rabbit made an amplificatory comment she really had to get off her chest. For her, the story of *Alice in Wonderland* fits with the dream events. It gives her, probably in some vague way, the feeling that for her the dream yields more when bounced off the image of Alice.

When we look at the story of *Alice's Adventures in Wonderland*, by Lewis Carroll, as amplificatory material for the underwater rabbit in George's dream, our attention falls on the images of the rabbit and of liquid. We skip the many other aspects of the story; otherwise we would end up with far too much material.

Alice finds the entrance to the wonderful world of Wonderland via the burrow of the white rabbit. When she has fallen to the heart of this world of imagination, she discovers a little vial of liquid. She drinks it and shrinks till she's only ten inches high. Then she becomes very big. She has arrived in a land of form-altering liquid. She cries and the liquid from her tears makes a big pool. Then she becomes small again and swims around in her bath of tears. In the pool of her own bitter tears, Alice meets the beings who live in this marvelous world of imagination. When questioned about her identity, Alice answers, "I know who I *was* this morning, but since then I have changed several times." In this world of imagination her identity gets lost. Alice also complains that she is losing her memory (just like in a dream world, where the images evaporate immediately).

"We are all mad in this world," says the Cheshire cat.

Elsewhere in the story, it is always six P.M. Tea time.

Through the white rabbit and her own tears, Alice has landed in a world of transformation, insanity, weak memory, and endless repetition.

The last meeting with the white rabbit, who brought her to this world in the depths, is in court. He appears to be the messenger of the king. (Mercury, who is called *psychopompos*, Guide of Souls, because he leads souls to the underworld, also is the messenger of the king of the gods. His Greek name is Hermes.) The court case, in which the queen has everyone's head chopped off, makes Alice so angry that she awakens from Wonderland. Ultimately, it seems that the white rabbit is connected to the murderous queen.

When we project the image world of Alice onto George's dream of the underwater rabbit, the following image arises:

In the heart of early childhood lives a rabbit who leads one to the depths, depths of constant transformation that one has to get in touch with. Habitual consciousness visits an underwater world of its own tears that makes most people lose their heads. The bloodthirsty female ruler of this world severs the head from the body. Here, the rabbit is the figure who causes the main character to fall into the depths of a world of oblivion. This is a role alchemy ascribes to *Mercurius psychopompos*, Mercury, who guides the souls of the dead to the underworld.

In the *Rosarium philosophorum* (digested by C. G. Jung in his book *Psychology of the Transference*), an alchemical text of 1550, there is an engraving of a round bowl filled with liquid. This engraving is called "Fount of Mercury."

The liquid is a blend of the essences of all the planets. Alchemy saw in the planets qualitatively distinct divine forces, the various dominant elements of divine *imagination*. This mixture of the combined creative potency of all the diverging cosmic forces was called *aqua vitae*, the water of life. In this bowl, filled with the cosmic liquid, is chaos, the unformed mixture of all vital force. This is the Hermetic vessel in which transformation, the changing of form, takes place.

Today this water of life is also called libido—sexual passion and passion for life. The rabbit, too, is often depicted as an extremely sexually passionate being. If we project these images like slides on top of the dream, the following image appears: In the round bowl full of liquid, all the potentials for the development of vital energy are intermingled. This confusion-enhancing state that brings everything into flux is of great potency; a strong potential in chaotic mixup, a vital and sexual passion that seethes in the heart and is connected with early childhood.

In French folk superstition there is the notion that eating rabbit meat is bad for the memory. The rabbit brings oblivion, as also became clear in *Alice*.

In many tales the rabbit and its alter ego the hare* are depicted as sly deceivers who cause culture to develop a step further. They are untrustworthy and dangerous helpers in the propagation of consciousness. This is also a role attributed to Mercury.

But who is this Mercury, who in his vessel constantly transmutes the passion for life?

———

*The symbolism of the hare and the rabbit is explored more fully by the Jungian analyst John Layard in *The Lady of the Hare: A Study in the Healing Power of Dreams* (Boston: Shambhala Publications, 1988). Coincidentally, Shambhala published *A Little Course in Dreams* simultaneously with Layard's book.

– 11 –

The Imagination as Healing Poison

Mercury harbors in his fount all forms of imagination—from the most demonic nightmare to the most divine vista. He is depicted as extremely untrustworthy and deceitful, a figure who is always throwing others off balance. He is the god of all those who are traveling, of everything that moves from one point to another. A god of transition, of the intermediate world, where he rules over scoundrels and thieves. A horny god, full of foul and dirty tricks. To alchemy, he was the savior. From this dark, untrustworthy, poisonous, and crafty being, the alchemist had to make the elixir, the remedy that consists of poison and of the poisoning that brings healing. They called it *pharmacon*, "healing poison."

Dreamwork is work on the imagination.

In the previous era, imagination was consigned to the world of artists and madmen. This narrow conception of the imagination leaves out of consideration the fact that imagination continually deforms and transforms our experience; that imagination plays a central role in perception, no matter how objective we think we are. Especially in dreams, it is clear how powerful the imagination is—it is capable of shaping a completely real world, indistinguishable from the physical world.

Our neuroses are illnesses of the imagination, Freud discovered. He found out that not only do traumas make us ill (a trauma is a terrible event that injures someone's soul or body or both), but so does our incestuous imagination (the Oedipus complex). We experience things in our imagination that are indistinguishable from the historical facts of our life. Early childhood in particular is a mixture of imagination and history.

For the alchemists it was of great importance that Mercury, god of imagination, not be loosed on the world in his crude form. They spoke of him as a storm bird, an impudent demon who incites humans to fury. They called him the "wild Mercury" who must be tamed. He reveals himself as a dragon and as a roaring lion. Wild Mercury manifests himself as the raw force of destruction that can dominate the imagination and have hideous effects on the world. He creates, among other things, the bloodthirsty frenzies of the Berserkers—the Germanic frenzy and ecstatic battle lust that was already called *furor teutonicus* before Tacitus (A.D. 55–120). This passionate urge to destroy was running riot in 1942 when Jung gave his Eranos lecture, "Der Geist Mercurius" (The Spirit Mercury). Jung spoke of the duplicity of the imagination, which on one hand can move us to love and deeds of healing beauty, and on the other hand to a frenzy of destruction that appears insane.

I always wondered why in 1942, in the middle of the war, Eranos occupied itself with Hermes/Mercurius. I now understand that it is of great political importance to recognize that archaic imagination in the form of mass mania can possess millions of people. Such recognition gives us the perspective of the archaic powers in the human imagination, archaic powers that did not in the least come to an end with the fall of Nazi Germany.

For his Eranos lecture of 1942, Jung took as his material "The Spirit in the Bottle," as told by the brothers Grimm. A poor peasant had a son who, for lack of money, was unable to complete his studies. This son found among the roots of an old oak a bottle, from which a voice was crying, "Let me out! Let me out!" The young peasant opened the bottle and a powerful spirit came out, as big as the oak. The spirit said, "I am the great and powerful Mercury. As a penance, I was shut up here. He who gives me freedom—his neck I must break." The young man came up with a trick. He said he didn't believe that such a great spirit could come out of such a little bottle; he wanted to see the feat with his own eyes. To prove it, Mercury went back into the bottle, whereupon the young man quickly replaced the stopper, and the spirit was imprisoned once again. He promised the young man a reward if he would set him free—a cloth that could turn whatever one rubbed into silver. The young man set the spirit free, received the cloth, turned his ax into silver, and got enough money for it to finish his studies. He became a famous doctor (*pharmacon*).

In his wild form, Mercury appears to be a mighty neck-breaker, a spirit of murderous passion bringing destruction; *pharmacon* as poison. Back in the bottle—in his refined form, the form contained by reflection, he turns base metal into reflecting silver—he is *pharmacon* as healing power. Mercury is the identity of bloodthirst and healing power. The bloodthirsty neck-breaker must be cheated in order to get to the reverse side of his identity. I imagine this deception to take place in dream craft. In dreams, heated desires and homicidal impulses surface. We let these images develop as if they actually could be indulged, as though the bloodthirsty and destructive impulses actually could be put into action. Then, at the last moment, we capture these shadow sides of Mercury in a reflection. In this way the image is entirely lived through but not acted out. Mercury, the revelation of darkness, is endured as an impulse cheated out of its action. In my dream about Angie, for example, it is important to experience the murderous, neck-biting bulldog without literally becoming this neck-biter. Identification with the bulldog would be fatal, but feeling the blood-thirsty dog through and through can become a remedy.

Thus it is apparently a matter of keeping the spirit of Mercury inside the bottle. In Ginger's dreams about the mud, we could clearly observe how such a bottle, such a Hermetic vessel, comes into being. After this series of dreams had taken place, Ginger executed a number of pieces with the mirror theme as a central image, as if the objective were to subject images to a process of reflection. Within a clearly delineated form, the vessel, imagination must be subjected to itself through a process of disciplined reflection. Through this process, a concentration of imaginative power takes place. The metaphorical force of an image is strengthened, and the compulsion to express the image directly in a literal way diminishes. This concentration of imagination heightens its potency and with it the healing, transformative power of Mercury, god of wondrous change.

For an example of concentrated imagination, let us return to the figure of the doctor in the airplane dream (see

Chapter 2). Stella meets the doctor after she falls into the dirty world, from which she has a hard time washing herself clean. After her crash Stella is in the grip of the sexual world.

No longer fleeing from sex, she can surrender to the healing libido—the exotic Doctor in White.

Stella's tolerance for the world of sex is going to be awakened by the doctor. This sexual involvement can take place on different levels. One of the possibilities, for example, is that this erotic image can be experienced in the transference to me, the analyst. In this case, Mercury remains inside the therapy, and the erotic drama takes place inside the bottle. It is also possible that Stella will now start having affairs with exotic men, affairs that will bring her in close contact with exotic masculine sexual passion. In this case, it will be much harder to keep Mercury in the bottle. The destructive power of imagination could easily run away with Stella, with disastrous results. One need only think of a talented gigolo who might seduce and deceive Stella, and many tragic scenarios could be imagined. Particularly in such a case, it is of great importance to apply concentrated reflection to the image of the sex doctor so that the metaphorical healing value of the image is not lost. Otherwise the dream image will not receive the intense penetration that it could have, and the sinister and deceitful Mercury might literally destroy her life. Mercury delights in causing the downfall of the I-figure through his cunning tricks.

At this point in history we can recognize the action of the two sides of Mercury in world events as well. The imagination has created a technology that concentrates the homicidal lust of Mercury into tools of total destruction. Along with the great beauty the technological imagination has created, it has fed the bloodthirsty neck-breaker, so that he is mightier now than ever.

With the advent of the nuclear threat, the art of Mercury, the intercourse with the imagination, should be practiced intensively. Otherwise our creativity might result in our destruction.

I believe the advent of the nuclear bomb is directly connected with the power of the imagination's archaic homicidal lust. In its raw form, this lust leads to total destruction, and it has now created the weapons that can accomplish it.

If we are convinced that "we" do not want this annihilation, we believe that the "other" plans our ruin. But neither "we" nor "they" want this destruction; the spirit of wild Mercury at the root of our imagination wants it. Now more than ever, it is vital to focus upon the raw urge to destruction that exists in the imagination. If we do not recognize this bloodthirst and feel it through to its depth, then Mercury may deceive us and subjugate us to a paranoid and deathly dread of the homicidal urge of our adversaries, whether they be communists or capitalists. This can be fatal.

On My Way Home

In the car on my way home. I'm tired after a long day and I'm driving pretty much on automatic pilot.

Today, during my afternoon nap, I had a dream.

I'm walking through a city that is unfamiliar to me. In the window of a furniture store I see some "Persian dogs." They look like reddish-purple bulldogs that could have been made out of porcelain in prehistoric times, were it not for the fact that they're alive. I look inside. One of the dogs, dressed in a brown suede suit, clearly a female animal, comes toward me. She's walking on her hind legs. On her reddish-purple face is a Salvador Dali–like mustache, burned in, as it were. Her porcelainlike head shines like a mirror. "This is impossible,″ I think to myself, "but that doesn't matter." She comes closer, and from behind the glass I hear her say. "Tell everybody, tell Peter . . ."

Then the alarm clock went off.

The dream immediately reminds me of Angie and the bulldog, whom I had seen at the beginning of this little course in dreams, during the initial dream. The beautiful, fantastic "Persian bulldog" bitch looks like a mixture of Angie and the bulldog that jumped at her throat. There she stands behind glass, as in a bottle, along with the other furniture in the interior design shop. She is alive and is at the same time an archaic image; she is surrealistic, with Dali's mustache burned into her porcelainlike head, in which I can almost see my own reflection. Her color is a blend of earthy blood and sky blue; the purple Persian dog. She has something to say to me. I also have changed. It doesn't matter to me anymore that things are happening that seem impossible. My rational consciousness lets itself be tripped with ease, like the kind of doll that returns to its upright position when pushed over.

Through working on this dream course, something has happened to me. The two manifestations of Mercury who were locked in mortal combat—one an inspiring female dog with the power to heal, the other a bloodthirsty, power-hungry male—have fused during this little course in dreams.

This phenomenon is what Jung calls the *transcendent function*. Behind this infelicitous term is hidden the idea that, if you process the opposites long enough without taking sides with one or the other, an *identity of opposites* can develop, as the alchemists would say.

The fundamental opposition in alchemy is portrayed by the tension between man and woman. Through the alchemical process, this tension can develop into the image of the hermaphrodite, the man-woman in whom the conflicting elements are unified so that a new identity has come into being. It seems as if the opposing elements have an identical root. Inside the bottle, one can penetrate to this root. *A Little Course in Dreams* was apparently such a bottle, a bottle in which the *prima materia*—the struggle between the healing and the bloodthirsty/power-hungry dogs of my imagination (a struggle understood by the alchemists as the inner conflict of the paradoxical Mercury)—could be fired and transformed into living, mirrorlike porcelain. The animal has been humanized; she walks upright and wears clothes. At the same time, the natural image of the Saint Bernard and the bulldog have been melted down and re-fused into a surrealistic, archaic image that has something to say to me.

"Tell everybody . . ." The identity "Angie-bulldog" wants to be heard by everyone. Oh, the lust for power, which compels the soul to expression. Without it, no book would be written, no ideas disseminated!

"Tell Peter . . ." I must immediately think of Peter, who bears the golden key in the favorite book of my childhood. He gave a little boy a silver key with which the imaginative power could be unlocked. Reflecting silver appears to give access to the world of healing power and nightmare—the dream world.

The car stops in front of my house.

Notes

1. C. G. Jung, *Memories, Dreams, Reflections*, recorded and edited by Aniela Jaffé, translated by Richard and Clara Winston (New York: Vintage Books, 1965), pp. 179, 181.
2. Henry Corbin, "*Mundus Imaginalis*, or the Imaginary and the Imaginal," *Spring 1972* (Dallas: Spring Publications, 1972), p. 9.
3. C. G. Jung, *Mysterium Coniunctionis*, in *Collected Works* 14 (Princeton, N.J.: Princeton University Press, Bollingen Series, 1953–1979), paragraph 307.
4. Ibid.
5. Robert Bosnak, "The Dirty Needle: Images of the Inferior Analyst," *Spring 1984* (Dallas: Spring Publications, 1984), p. 105.